D1489877

NEW ORLEANS GOES TO THE MOVIES

NEW ORLEANS GOES TO THE MOVIES

FILM SITES IN THE FRENCH QUARTER AND BEYOND

Alan T. Leonhard

Illustrations by Jason LeBlanc

Margaret Media, Inc.

Published by Margaret Media, Inc.

Copyright © 2008 Alan T. Leonhard

Cover by Jason LeBlanc   Book design by Molly Ebert

ISBN 978-0-9616377-9-8

Printed in the U.S.A. by
Sheridan Books, Chelsea, Michigan

Library of Congress Cataloging-in-Publication Data

Leonhard, Alan T.
 New Orleans goes to the movies : film sites in the French Quarter and beyond / Alan T. Leonhard ; illustrations by Jason LeBlanc.
    p. cm.
 Includes bibliographical references and index.
 ISBN 978-0-9616377-9-8 (alk. paper)
 1. Motion picture locations--Louisiana--New Orleans. 2. New Orleans (La.)--In motion pictures. I. Title.
 PN1995.67.N64L46 2008
 791.43'6358763--dc22
                            2008038564

Margaret Media, Inc.
618 Mississippi Street
Donaldsonville, LA 70346
(225) 473-9319
www.margaretmedia.com

ACKNOWLEDGMENTS

I am grateful to Sylvia Kennen for her assistance during the drafts and re-drafts of the manuscript. Mary Gehman helped tirelessly with suggestions for improvements. In the early states of research, John Magill of the Historic New Orleans Collection steered me toward many resources for the project. Dave Roberts provided valuable comments on the text and Molly Ebert provided technical help on the final product.

TO SHELBY, BARRETT, JACK,
REESE, AND ABIGAIL

TABLE OF CONTENTS

ILLUSTRATIONS

ILLUSTRATIONS CONTINUED

French Quarter Carriage Ride

INTRODUCTION

Most first time visitors to New Orleans have fixed ideas about the city based upon what they saw in movie theaters. Many big screen images of New Orleans can be traced to numerous films shot or set in the French Quarter and other sections of the city. This book proposes to show why Hollywood chose the city for so many productions. To journey through the French Quarter and other historic places, read about them, or see a film shot on location is a pleasurable experience. Films lure visitors and locals to an ambience rooted in the city's distinctive mixture of cultures, languages, music, art and religions. Directors have been inspired by writers and painters to capture scenes in historically preserved places. Many moviemakers consider settings that are visually powerful for audiences. We are given a glimpse into the past even though films tend to romanticize stories about the city. How did people in New Orleans in the 18th, 19th, and early 20th centuries live? The answer might lead us to discover why New Orleans is considered "America's Most Interesting City."

Twenty films representing various genres and historic eras were selected to give the reader access to a wide range of movies and personal preferences.

At the back of the book there are tours and maps

of selected film sites in the French Quarter and beyond. This allows individuals to compare locations with images formed by them as filmgoers. Set designers, camera crews, directors, and everyone else working on a motion picture make decisions about how to use a cinema site. Cinema directors decide as to how much of a picture will be shot on location or at a Hollywood studio. The chapters are organized into film genres and historical eras. Whenever possible the reader will be told about how many sequences in a movie were filmed on location or on a set.

A complete list of movies included is as follows: *Interview With the Vampire* (1994), *The Feast of All Saints* (2003), *The Buccaneer* (1958), *Jezebel* (1938), *Saratoga Trunk* (1945), *New Orleans* (1947), *Pretty Baby* (1978), *The Cincinnati Kid* (1965), *Walk on the Wild Side* (1962), *Blaze* (1989), *Panic in the Streets* (1950), *A Streetcar Named Desire* (1951), *Easy Rider* (1969), *Cat People* (1982), *JFK* (1991), *Double Jeopardy* (1999), *King Creole* (1959), *The Big Easy* (1987), *The Pelican Brief* (1993), and *Runaway Jury* (2003). Some are based upon a book or a play. Others follow a screenplay script. All use New Orleans as settings in portions of the pictures.

The French Quarter, also called the Vieux Carré (Old Square), attracts millions of visitors a year. It is from this living museum with a large inventory of historic architecture in both its public and private buildings that many images of New Orleans arise. It is a six by thirteen rectangular square block section dating back to colonial times when the French (1718-1762) and Spanish (1762-1803) ruled the Louisiana Territory. It was returned to the French, and in 1803, Napoleon sold it to the United States. The colonial period gave it a European look which continued to exist under American rule. Its lifestyle and unique buildings remained when descendants of the French, Spanish and Africans of the colonial times continued to inhabit this enclave. Others from the Caribbean and Europe settled here. They were joined by immigrants from Europe. It was a melting pot even when it witnessed a decline into a slum and remained "foreign." A powerful preservation movement in the twentieth century helped protect the area from several modern encroachments.

In guide books it is described as exotic, decadent, like no other place in America, magnificent, European, African, Caribbean, hedonistic, a bohemia, colorful, sensory, historic, and Roman Catholic. It comes as no surprise that Hollywood continues to use the place as a site for cinematic productions on studio lots and on location.

In a time frame the films discussed in this book range from *Jezebel* in 1938 to *The Feast of All Saints* in 2003. Both movies used very expensive sets aimed at re-creating New Orleans in the mid and early 1800s.

The first is praised for a representation of the Old South. The second is based on Anne Rice's novel of the same name. *Jezebel* contains many themes from Old South mythology. Mint juleps, plantation life and a code of honor based on dueling appear frequently. But the 1853 yellow fever epidemic in New Orleans fills the narrative as the love story between the principal characters Julie Marsden (Bette Davis) and Preston Dillard (Henry Fonda) plays out. *The Feast of All Saints* covers the free people of color as a people in peril in nineteenth century New Orleans. The two movies will be discussed later.

For now, it is important to define the boundaries of the area of the city where the twenty films were shot on location or on a set. The six by thirteen grid of the Quarter and several blocks adjacent to it along the curve of the Mississippi River and along Basin Street (see the map at the back) will be included in the discussion of sites. The river front and St. Louis #1 Cemetery appear in some of the pictures and should be mentioned as places favored by filmmakers. A long, fascinating history, lush greenery and flowers, beautiful architecture, scenic streets, promenade on the river, and other aesthetic aspects in the area offer the camera special visual effects. The St. Charles Avenue and Garden District section of the city has also been used by Hollywood to portray New Orleans in movies and will be part of our description of movie sites.

Hollywood should be thanked for building replicas on studio sets of two French Quarter landmarks. The French Opera House and the old St. Louis Hotel appear in films covered on the tour. In *Jezebel* and *Saratoga Trunk* the interiors of the French Opera House and the St. Louis Hotel are shown even though these structures no longer exist. One burned beyond repair (the Opera House) and the other was demolished (the St. Louis Hotel). Both symbolized the "joy of life" culture in the old Quarter. Later an attempt will be made to describe these two venerable buildings, which disappeared early in the twentieth century, and in the chapters covering *Jezebel* and *Saratoga Trunk* the two historic buildings will be discussed.

Two tours and two maps at the back of the book will help us find film sites in New Orleans. One tour covers the French Quarter. The second uses the St. Charles Avenue streetcar to view movie sites and other points of interest along the way. The sketches throughout the book help us recognize historic structures on the tours. Some illustrations help us visualize how New Orleans may have appeared in earlier times. Sets used by filmmakers try to replicate New Orleans during early times. The illustrations and text attempt to give filmgoers other means to judge Hollywood's visions of this magical city.

Napoleon House

CHAPTER 1

WHY NEW ORLEANS HAS ATTRACTED FILMS

William Faulkner and Tennessee Williams are among the great writers who strolled around the French Quarter streets seeking and receiving inspiration for their works. Movie fans can walk in the same place looking for film sites in this book. While traveling through older parts of the city bear in mind that both Faulkner and Williams worked as scriptwriters in Hollywood and surely learned a great deal about the appeal of films. Both writers needed money in the periods when they were employed by motion picture studios. While living in the French Quarter they had to struggle to lift themselves out of poverty. In the late 1920s and early 1930s many authors were attracted to the unconventional life in the Quarter which at that time was an immigrant slum. It was a refuge where rent and food were cheap and where alcoholic drinks were abundant, even during Prohibition. The old rundown neighborhood was carefree and fun-loving. It was often described as a Caribbean enclave in North America. Situated in a semitropical seaport city the sense of place was exotic and foreign. With its French origins and Spanish architecture the Quarter was closely tied to its colonial past.

This bohemian atmosphere was fertile ground for creative people in the arts and literature. By 1910, the Quarter was eighty percent Sicilian. This wave of immigrants transformed this oldest city neighborhood into a Latin ghetto populated by a new cultural group which showed a great tolerance for eccentricity. The French Market built by the Spanish was now occupied by seafood, meat, fruit and vegetable vendors from Italy. By many accounts even goats and chickens lived in courtyards, apartments and houses along with their owners. Roman Catholicism was still the predominant religion and French Creoles both white and of color continued living along with the new immigrants, creating a potpourri in language and traditions more common to the West Indies than North America.

Sherwood Anderson, a well-known writer who lived in one of the Pontalba buildings on Jackson Square, encouraged promising writers to live in the South's new literary enclave. William Faulkner was to become his most famous recruit.

While living in a room overlooking St. Anthony's Garden behind St. Louis Cathedral Faulkner wrote his first novel, **Soldiers' Pay**, published articles in local newspapers and contributed essays to the prestigious literary journal **The Double Dealer** which was published in New Orleans. Other famous figures in literature of the era who visited the Quarter were Ernest Hemingway, Thornton Wilder, Gertrude Stein, Thomas Wolfe, and New Orleans-born Truman Capote.

One story involving William Faulkner told on a literary tour of the Quarter is about the author being described in an old guidebook as making a living leading tour groups. It can be traced to a time when some of his close friends who ran a travel company were asked by the Chamber of Commerce to hire guides to show conventioneers the sights in part of the old section. The friends knew about Faulkner's firsthand knowledge of the history and architecture of the Quarter. They used him and several other guides. The visitors were divided into groups about one block apart. Faulkner's imaginative mind caused him to make up fantastic tales about places along the route. At one point most of the conventioneers drifted from other groups as they heard the natural storyteller's accounts of what mysterious events took place in various buildings as he wandered through the narrow streets and alleys. In one of his essays written later, he expressed his love of New Orleans by describing the city as: "A courtesan, not old and yet no longer young, who shuns the sunlight that the illusion of her former glory be preserved."

Tennessee Williams was also charmed by a city which he called his "spiritual home." Williams began to live in the Quarter in 1938. He hoped that some of his plays would be supported by the Federal Writers Project in New Orleans, sponsored by the Works Project Administration, with the goal of helping struggling writers with their creative pursuits. Ironically, Williams, the figure who put the city on the literary map, was not helped by the Writers Project. He made a living by waiting tables at restaurants and even hocked his typewriter in despair. Both Faulkner and Williams were inspired by the Quarter and New Orleans, and returned frequently to the place as they evolved into two of America's most highly respected writers.

At different junctures in their careers, they were employed as scriptwriters for studios in Hollywood. Those experiences surely had an impact on the evolution in writing styles for which they received international acclaim. Perhaps to know what moviegoers wanted to see in films gave each important insights into crafting some of their future works. The jobs did give each salaries to rescue them from monetary troubles and allowed them to concentrate on completing novels, plays, and other literary pieces. Faulkner worked on at least twenty-seven screenplays on and off from the 1930s until the 1950s at three Hollywood studios. Perhaps the most widely known of his screenplays is an adaptation of Ernest Hemingway's novel *To Have and Have Not* (1944). This picture was the first to feature Humphrey Bogart and Lauren Bacall, a couple whose presence on the screen and their private lives became legendary. Faulkner was befriended by the filmmaker Howard Hawks who had read his first novel *Solders' Pay* and introduced him to key figures in the publishing business in New York.

Several movies are based upon Faulkner's novels and short stories. *The Long Hot Summer* (1958) from *The Hamlet* and starring Paul Newman, Joanne Woodward, and Orson Wells is known best by movie fans. *Intruder in the Dust* (1949), *The Sound and the Fury* (1959), *Sanctuary* (1961), and *The Reivers* (1969) are other films based on his writings. When Faulkner was living in New Orleans his patron, Sherwood Anderson, took long walks with him around the French Quarter and riverfront. Anderson advised him to continue to concentrate on fiction and what he knew best, i.e. Mississippi and his hometown Oxford. The rest is history because this advice brought him great success.

Tennessee Williams also used the South as a locale for his works but stated that New Orleans was the source for the majority of his material. An emotional attachment to the city continued throughout his life. Williams' agent, Audrey Wood, got him a screen writing job at MGM in Hollywood. At least fifteen films were made from plays, novels, and other Williams' original sources. The movie *A Streetcar Named Desire* (1951) came from his Pulitzer Prize play. He completed this play while living in a third story apartment in the French Quarter where he could hear the rattling streetcar rolling along a nearby street.

After *A Streetcar Named Desire* appeared on the screen, Williams was accorded celebrity status. Vivien Leigh, Kim Hunter, and Karl Malden received Oscars for their performances and another Oscar went to the film for art direction. Marlon Brando was nominated, but the Oscar went to Humphrey Bogart for *The African Queen*. Brando, who at the time was a virtual unknown in Hollywood, would emerge at a "star" in future roles. Williams became the best known playwright in cinema and he continued to draw upon New Orleans for plays and films. In a later chapter, *A Streetcar Named Desire* will be discussed at length.

The special appeal of the French Quarter as a place can be seen in the stories set in old New Orleans in the 1880s and 1890s by Lafcadio Hearn, George Washington Cable and other writers in the post-Civil War period. What cultural historians call the "culture of defeat" contributed to a renaissance in literature about the South and New Orleans. Also, pioneers in Hollywood saw the box-office profits soar when films became a form of escape for moviegoers from the harsh realities of life to the idyllic times of the Old South. *Jezebel* (1938) captures the prosperous times of New Orleans in the 1850s as a city surrounded by plantations. Julie Marsden (Bette Davis), the central character in the picture owns a mansion in the city and a plantation nearby. The conniving Southern belle defies social conventions by appearing at a party in a riding outfit and later at a ball in a red dress. Her social circle dictated that single women wear white dresses to Mardi Gras balls. In dark theaters around the country audiences admired her defiant spirit. What existed in the past or is imagined to have existed is a powerful theme on the big screen.

What draws viewers to this time period? One answer to this is seen in the fact that the South and New Orleans in antebellum times were isolated from the rest of America. The region created a culture tied to the mythology of a way of life tied to a thriving plantation system and port city.

The symbolism of the Old South flourished long after the Civil War. In Williams' *A Streetcar Named Desire* Blanche DuBois personifies how many people were still clinging to what existed in the past and was then not only in decline but in decay. Movie fans and Hollywood found a lasting infatuation with "southern agrarianism."

In contrast with Julie in *Jezebel*, Blanche comes to New Orleans to live with her sister in a slum apartment in the French Quarter. In *Jezebel*, Julie and other women in high society are treated as "chalices to be cherished and protected." Blanche, even in her tarnished state, struggles to maintain the manners and style of a fading belle from the Mississippi Delta when she encounters the animalistic Stanley.

In all the pictures covered in subsequent chapters New Orleans is a location favored by moviemakers. Its colonial architecture, houses with carriageways and patios, and historic aura give a sense of the past. Borrowing a phrase from the classic mystery film *The Maltese Falcon* New Orleans is a place filled with "the stuff that dreams are made of."

Having said that New Orleans is filled with "the stuff that dreams are made of," the person who embodies these dreams most is Anne Rice. She was born there and educated in Catholic schools in the city. Rice has written twenty-eight novels, many drawing upon the city's mysteries and history. She is by far the most popular and prolific contemporary fiction-author from New Orleans.

When she and her husband Stan moved from California to New Orleans in 1989, they bought a Greek Revival home in the Garden District in the Uptown section of the city. The Italianate mansion is a character in some of her novels. While here, Anne Rice wrote screenplays for films based on her works. Two of these movies are examined in this book, *Interview With the Vampire* and *The Feast of All*

Saints are found in Chapters two and three.

Interview With the Vampire on the screen takes us through the supernatural world while visiting New Orleans from colonial times to the present. It spans the ages and allows us to experience history over two centuries. Anne Rice has a special ability to entice fans to think about the past. The picture will become a classic in the horror genre for Hollywood.

The Feast of All Saints is a fictional work taking us into the real lives of the free people of color in Louisiana. During the slave revolt in Haiti in the early 1800s, thousands of free people of color came to Louisiana. They brought with them the French language and a cultural heritage unique to North America. We see how these people adjusted to a new life through the characters in the story.

Anne Rice, with an eye on preservation, purchased and renovated several properties in the Garden District. This dedication to the past is crucial to making New Orleans a prime destination for visitors who value historical structures as connections to former days. Like the characters in Rice's novels and movies based upon her works in literature, we find ourselves as participants in her stories while journeying through the old sections of the city in a quest for bygone times. We can combine the images seen in films with the history that surrounds us on the French Quarter and St. Charles Avenue tours found at the back of the book. Anne Rice utilizes New Orleans as a place for her tales about the supernatural world and real life. It is fortunate that she and other preservationists did so much to maintain a legacy for the future.

Madame John's Legacy

CHAPTER 2

THE COLONIAL PERIOD– 1718-1810

INTERVIEW WITH THE VAMPIRE (1994)

In 1791, Louis (Brad Pitt) in the movie *Interview With the Vampire* expresses his desire to go to Paris: "it comes not only from reading of all the literature and philosophy, but from the feeling of having been shaped by Europe more deeply and keenly than the rest of Americans. I was a Creole who wanted to see where it all began."

To understand New Orleans' history, one should divide the past with a broad range of dates. The original city was founded by Bienville in 1718 and dominated by the Creoles until 1810. The term "Creole" is a derivative of *criollo,* a Spanish term referring to people born in the New World of European ancestry (usually with parents from France or Spain). In New Orleans, it was applied to Europeans embracing the French language, French culture, and the Roman Catholic religion.

As will be described in the next chapter, "Creole" was expanded to include the free people of color, *(les gens de couleur libre)* persons of African descent who also adopted the French language, culture, and Roman Catholicism.

The movie ***Interview With the Vampire***, based on Anne Rice's novel, gives us a remarkable visual portrait of what it may have been like to live in New Orleans during colonial times. Louis (Brad Pitt) in 1791 is in mourning over the deaths in his family. His grief as a survivor is unbearable. Social and economic status places him in the *crème de la crème* of aristocratic society. He owns a large plantation on River Road and a townhouse in the French Quarter. His friends are also wealthy Creoles who entertain on a lavish level with soirees at their plantation homes and in the city. Lestat (Tom Cruise) observes his despair and offers him the alternative of vampire immortality to replace a life filled with sorrow over the loss of his family.

In 1788, while under Spanish rule, the Vieux Carré burned to the ground in what was called the "Good Friday fire." Over 856 public and private buildings were destroyed. The Spanish authorities implemented a strict fire code that included new types of roofs and buildings extending to the sidewalks (called *banquettes* in French because the original wooden walkways resembled benches). Interior courtyards were built for practical and aesthetic reasons. Many courtyards had fountains and gardens. The French Quarter became Spanish in design resembling cities like Seville.

As you walk the route in this book, you will see street signs in English and in French on the light posts (Royal Street and *Rue Royale)*. Spain ruled the colony for nearly forty years. In 1959, the Spanish Government gave the city beautiful glazed tiles bearing street names in Spanish to represent that era. The multicolored attractive tiles attached to buildings at eye level at almost every corner in the Vieux Carré appeal to people walking through the historic Quarter. Royal Street is *Calle Real* on the tiles. These tiles represent Spanish colonial rule in Louisiana from 1762 until 1803.

Madame John's Legacy (a West Indies style house named for a fictitious character) at 632 Dumaine Street was the site in **Interview With the Vampire** for the haunting scene in the movie when coffins were carried down from the second story veranda to antique hearses decorated with black ostrich plumes and pulled by white horses. Before shooting this sequence, the production company dumped loads of mud in front of Madame John's Legacy and on Royal Street for several blocks to replicate the Vieux Carré in the eighteenth century. Jackson Square and the Cabildo with its multiple arches and elaborate ironwork appear in the film in scenes when Lestat (Tom Cruise) is roaming the Quarter in search of victims. The Cabildo sequence used fog machines for dramatic purposes but the building still has the sensational appearance of old colonial times. The power of Hollywood's special effects on the big screen is highlighted throughout the film in many scenes.

Another historic property on the walking tour is the Gallier House Museum at 1132 Royal. It was used as a model for Louis (Brad Pitt) and Lestat's (Tom Cruise) townhouse by the art director in the film. The movie was nominated in 1994 for an Academy Award for Best Art Director.

The waterfront scenes with sailing vessels and dark muddy docks on the river are very striking to viewers with an avid interest in the occult world of vampires and how the French Quarter may have appeared in colonial times. This part of the film was shot at Jackson Barracks, downriver from the Quarter. In post-production, any modern structures such as metal towers with power lines or the two bridges upriver were covered with images of the masts of sailing ships to give moviegoers a sense of the period.

The everyday fear of numerous diseases is portrayed when the young girl Claudia (Kirsten Dunst) is rescued from the arms of her dead mother. Yellow fever, malaria and other tropical infectious illnesses plagued the first inhabitants on a daily basis. Rats were abundant as in any port city and provided the vampires with a steady diet as alternatives to humans.

The orphan, Claudia, becomes Louis and Lestat's

vampire companion after Lestat bites her on the neck and sucks blood from her body. When Louis and Claudia realize the power Lestat has over them, they try to kill him by setting him afire and dumping his remains in a swamp where they watch alligators devour his corpse. Then, they run to a sailing vessel docked on the river departing for Paris. The narrative by Louis includes : "I was Creole and it (Paris) was the mother of New Orleans."

He leaves behind him a plantation he has burned to the ground after his slaves discover that he is a vampire. Both Oak Alley and Destrehan plantations on River Road, north of New Orleans, were utilized as sets in the movie whenever his Pointe du Lac Plantation is shown from its interior and exterior. For example, there is a scene of Louis and Lestat sitting in an opulent plantation dining room being served by a strikingly beautiful young slave woman wearing an elaborate multi-toned Caribbean gown and headdress.

When Louis (Brad Pitt) returns to New Orleans from his travels in Europe, where he finds no solutions to his immortality as a vampire, he discovers Lestat (Tom Cruise) still alive after two hundred years in an eerie residence in a shriveled condition sitting in a foul-smelling chair in the dark. The locale is 1519 Esplanade Avenue known to local historians and architects as the Marsoudet-Caruso House. Lestat is covering his face to avoid lights from helicopters circling the house outside. Louis, who has adapted to modern life, assures him that it is artificial light that cannot harm him.

Individuals watching **Interview With the Vampire** can see Anne Rice's book come to life in a powerful way. In the visual world, the camera is able to paint lifelike figures in the demonic vampire cult. The Vieux Carré has a dark side capable of sweeping the audience up into a state of suspense and horror. The film also uses the swamps and haunting night scenes to heighten emotions moved by the macabre story.

Filmgoers and bibliophiles as well as the author herself go on record praising the movie for its excellence. For example, Rice was hesitant about the casting of Tom Cruise as Lestat because of his roles in previous films. Neil Jordon, the Oscar-winning director and others showed confidence in Cruise's versatility. When Rice saw him in screen tests acting from scripts based on her most famous novel, she was extremely pleased. The actor brought star power to the movie and was talented enough to take on a very challenging role. Brad Pitt as "Louis" and Christian Slater as "Daniel" the journalist both distinguished themselves as top performers. These three actors along with Antonio Banderas contributed greatly to its box-office success.

By targeting young people in the late teens and

early twenties (an age group known for frequent movie attendance), the filmmakers were confident that the picture would be a blockbuster. A budget of approximately fifty million dollars was well spent. With a generous budget, the production team was able to elevate the artistic aspects of the story on the screen. Anne Rice disciples from all age groups seemed to respond enthusiastically to the screen version of the book.

The Vieux Carré and Paris provide locales where the storyline plays out brilliantly. The Paris Opera House and various scenic walks on the Rue de Rivoli are spellbinding sights, as is New Orleans, with its European architecture and old cemeteries.

We did not live in the Vieux Carré in colonial times, but when we read written accounts about conditions in those days, the film *Interview With the Vampire* offers us a glance into that period. It is fiction and fantasy but every possible effort was made by the filmmakers to create a sense of time and place. Research shows that the privileged upper class exploited their status in colonial times to the maximum. The wealthy few certainly defined the social and cultural rules at that time, but the film also covers the harsh realities of slavery, disease, and abject poverty. To understand the world of today, it is necessary to reflect upon the past. Louis travels through time with the moviegoers. Technical innovations in special effects by Hollywood make this picture an educational venture.

Location, location, location! San Francisco, one of America's most majestic cities, is a well-chosen place for Louis to tell his tale about his trek from New Orleans to Paris and back to the interviewer. When Christian Slater becomes part of the plot as he and Lestat struggle on San Francisco's Golden Gate Bridge, film buffs are enticed into identifying more closely with the characters. Visitors who walk through the French Quarter or take a tour to Oak Alley or Destrehan plantations will experience a heightened awareness of colonial history in New Orleans by combining this excursion with what they may have remembered from the movie (plantation tours can be booked at local hotels).

CHAPTER 3

THE FREE PEOPLE OF COLOR – 1809-1850S

THE FEAST OF ALL SAINTS (2003)

"Yet in their shadowy world, between the white and the black, an aristocracy arose among them. Artists, poets, sculptors and musicians emerged, men and women of wealth, education and distinction.... And in their midst there existed always a species of beautiful woman whose allure for the well-to-do white men of Louisiana became a legend." This was the world of *les gens de couleur libre* described in Anne Rice's novel ***The Feast of All Saints***.

The Vieux Carré from 1762 until 1803 could be called the Spanish Quarter (although it is not given this name in the literature) because in those four decades under Spanish colonial rule so many residences and public buildings were rebuilt after the great fire of 1788. The Cabildo, the Cathedral, and even the French Market are the focal points in the French Quarter even though these structures are more Spanish than French in architectural style. Nonetheless, New Orleans remained French in culture, language and religion. The Spanish officials married French-speaking women

Bourbon Orleans Hotel

and instruction in schools remained French. The first newspaper, *Moniteur de la Louisiane*, was in French.

In the late 1700s and early 1800s, wave after wave of immigrants embracing this language and culture poured into the port city. The Acadians, expelled from their homes and farms by the British in 1755 in *Acadie* (now Nova Scotia) whose exodus was immortalized in Henry Wadsworth Longfellow's epic poem *Evangeline* began arriving in Louisiana in the 1760s through the 1780s. Most moved to the territory west of New Orleans called Acadiana, the center of Cajun culture, around present-day Lafayette. Then in the early 1800s, those fleeing the slave revolt in Haiti (St. Domingue), doubled the city's population. Many who fled were slave-owners.

The Feast of All Saints, another film based on a novel by native New Orleanian, Anne Rice, traces the origins of this last group. The refugee group from Haiti was made up of one-third Europeans, one-third free people of color *(les gens de couleur libre)*, and one-third slaves. Like other layers of French-speaking groups from Canada, Europe, and the Caribbean, the Haitians brought new customs, wealth, skills, dialects, and styles of cuisine to New Orleans.

Officials and plantation owners feared that the Haitian struggle would inspire slave revolts in Louisiana. Most slaves already in the area were descendants of people brought here from Senegambia in West Africa. A bloody slave uprising in 1811 reached the outskirts of New Orleans before it was put down. Twenty-three slaves were killed and their heads placed on poles along the River Road as a warning against future revolts.

As seen in Chapter Two, "Creole" is a derivative of the Spanish word *criollo*. It first applied to persons born in the New World of European ancestry, mainly of Spanish or French parentage. The French West Indies pre-dated the Louisiana colony by two-hundred years. The most famous Creole born in the islands was Marie Josèphine de la Pagarie from Martinique. Her first husband, Alexandre, Vicomte de Beauharnais, was executed during the French Revolution. Later, she met and married Napoleon Bonaparte. During an exhibit at the New Orleans Museum of Art, "Napoleon's France and Jefferson's America," her life was shown as a journey from Martinique to Malmaison.

What existed in Louisiana in the early 1800s was a three tiered society, i.e. European Creoles, free Creoles of color and French-speaking slaves. Miscegenation between European and Africans reinforced this social pattern. *The Feast of All Saints* dramatizes how the three groups interacted with a keen awareness about their respective positions. All three clung to the French language and culture. The film simplifies the complex rules setting boundaries among the groups.

For example, we see free people of color owning slaves and treating them with cruelty. At the same time, slaves yearned to enjoy the rights accorded to free people of color, e.g. possession of property.

European Creoles resisted the inclusion of people with African blood into the social class termed "Creole." Governor Miro, in 1786, in response to anger by white Creole women passed the *tignon* law under which it became a crime for women with African blood to wear fashionable clothes or headdresses with feathers or jewels on them. The law forced them to adorn their heads with kerchiefs like those worn by slave women. It did not work because many women of mixed African, European and Indian blood were so naturally beautiful that the scarves accentuated their exquisite facial features. Colonial European men were often more attracted to them than to white Creole women.

The free black community reinforced its dedication to education, music, fine food, architecture, and professional pursuits. Several families amassed fortunes in real estate in the Vieux Carré. In *The Feast of All Saints*, Marcel (Robert Ri'chard), the son of a white sugar planter and a free woman of color, is a product of the *plaçage* system. Under *plaçage*, eligible free women of color, chaperoned by mothers and aunts, attended the Quadroon balls at various places in the French Quarter. The so-called Quadroon Ballroom was at the Bourbon Orleans Hotel, 717 Orleans Ave. (Local legend says that "quadroon balls" were held here but there is no historical evidence that this is true.)

European Creole men paid admission to these elegant balls shown in **The Feast of All Saints**. By tradition, these Creole men usually waited until they reached financial standing in a business or profession before entering into matrimony. Since it took several years to gain this status some were thirty or more years old by that time. In the interim period, many entered into a contract or *plaçage* with free women of color. This was a verbal contract specifying the rights given to the mistress or *placée*. These might include a house, living expenses for life, and monetary trusts for children born to the couple. In some cases, the couple remained together for life (a de facto if not legal marriage). Others might be terminated if the man married a European woman. Some men maintained two families.

There are episodes in the film showing how contracts were drafted by a lawyer (despite the fact that no such documents have been located by contemporary researchers). The movie also gives the audience an idea about the elegance and formality, characteristic of the quadroon balls.

Marcel (Robert Ri'chard) is baffled as he searches for his identity in a situation with a father living on a sugar plantation with his second family and still spending time at Marcel's mother's home on Rue St. Ann in the Vieux Carré. He is puzzled by many historic events, particularly the slave revolt in Haiti. He agonizes over the ancient and evil institution of slavery while witnessing the sale of humans on an auction block. Marcel as an old man (James Earl Jones) gives a powerful performance while telling his life story from his photography studio. The actor's deep, melodious voice is spellbinding as he recounts how he learned the techniques used by the daguerreotype camera from a neighbor. His mother, Cecile Ste. Marie (Gloria Reuben), had been eager to send him to Paris to be educated but his father, Philippe (Peter Gallagher), died before her wish could be fulfilled.

The diaspora from Haiti by way of Cuba, Guadeloupe, and other islands, reached a high point of 10,000 refugees coming to New Orleans. In 1809 alone, thirty-four ships disgorged passengers by the thousands in this exodus to the port city. The first American governor, William C.C. Claiborne (1803-1816), tried to stem the tide of new arrivals as he grappled with the Spanish and French inhabitants still loyal to their respective mother countries. His government was also threatened by the British invasion in 1815. The Battle of New Orleans nearly resulted in a British capture of the city.

One can use **The Feast of All Saints** as a historical picture about the most turbulent period in the evolution of the Vieux Carré . Francophones from African, French, Spanish, and Caribbean roots converged to produce a unique culture still existing from that mix in race, customs, architectural designs and skills. Marcel as a young man (Robert Ri'chard) takes us through his personal odyssey in that era. Other actors in the movie include Jennifer Beals, Ossie Davis, and Ben Vareen. Eartha Kitt takes on the role of a voodoo priestess. Marie Laveau, a real life figure in the French Quarter, is most likely the inspiration for Kitt's mysterious persona.

In Chapter 6 dealing with the picture **Saratoga Trunk**, we will revisit the lives of generations in the Creole community so deeply embedded in the fabric of the Vieux Carré.

Andrew Jackson

CHAPTER 4

THE AMERICANIZATION ERA – 1803-1840

THE BUCCANEER (1958)

In the last chapter, reference was made to the formidable problems confronting the first American governor of Louisiana, William C.C. Claiborne. This was made in connection with the city's population doubling in one year as refugees from the Haitian slave rebellion flocked here. This same revolt ended Napoleon Bonaparte's ambition to restore the French Empire in North America. Thomas Jefferson sent high-ranking envoys to Paris in an attempt to buy New Orleans. Spain retroceded the Louisiana Territory back to France in 1800 in a secret treaty. At this time, Napoleon was challenging his greatest enemy, Great Britain, both on the Continent and in the New World. Failing to achieve complete dominance over Europe, he looked elsewhere to weaken Britain's power over the seas.

Americans during the Spanish colonial rule prospered by transporting goods on flatboats from the rich farmlands in the Midwest through the port of

New Orleans. Jefferson was keenly aware of this trade when he said

> "There is on this globe one single spot, the possessor of which is our natural and habitual enemy.... That is New Orleans."

Much to his surprise, Napoleon offered to sell the entire Louisiana Territory for fifteen million dollars. The fifteen million dollars paid for the Louisiana Purchase was not authorized by Congress. The U.S. Government had to borrow money from a British bank since it was in debt. The Louisiana Purchase Treaty was ratified by the Senate seven months after it was signed. In the first months, it is significant to note that the news about the acquisition of what domestic critics termed "a vast wilderness" shocked President Jefferson's opponents.

Napoleon lost over 25,000 troops from the army trying to put down the revolt in Haiti (San Domingue). The same army sent to fight Toussaint L'Ouverture on that island was supposed to go on to Louisiana under General Victor Emmanuel Leclerc's (Napoleon's brother-in-law) command but the expeditionary force was virtually exterminated in the jungles by the rebels or tropical fevers (including Leclerc).

In 1803, the Louisiana Territory was officially French again for twenty days when Pierre Clement Laussat was declared Colonial Prefect by Napoleon.

The Creoles in The Place d'Armes (now Jackson Square) in New Orleans cheered when the tricolor rose on the flagpole. Then the French colors were lowered and replaced with the American flag when Laussat turned the Territory over to Claiborne. The Creoles were aghast since the stereotype of Americans came from their encounters with the "Kaintucks." While in port, the hard-drinking, brawling, womanizing river-boatmen frequented the infamous section known as "the Swamp" several blocks from the riverfront docks upriver from the French Quarter. The stage was set for extended antagonism between Creoles and Americans.

Many problems confronted Governor Claiborne, not the least of which being a society so diverse and alien to the Anglo-Protestant new republic. He had to assure the Ursuline nuns that their Roman Catholic beliefs would continue without hindrance from his government because the nuns wrote a letter to Jefferson expressing their concerns about the future.

Cultural, racial and linguistic diversity befuddled new arrivals and visitors from the United States. From the French Market came a "babble of tongues" as shoppers from the Gallic-Caribbean society and foreigners in port gathered to examine a cornucopia of foods, spices, Indian baskets, and items never seen before by the Americans. Claiborne, a Virginian Protestant, could not speak French and was treated as a stranger when he relied on interpreters to implement new laws. He described the populace as one preoccupied with nightly balls who showed no concern about becoming good citizens. His first and second wives, daughter, and close friends died during outbreaks of yellow fever. In despair he looked at the filthy, disease-ridden streets from his house as he grappled with a town inhabited by disorderly masses.

Around the same time, Jean Lafitte, the legendary pirate, became wealthy by engaging in the illegal slave trade and selling loot from ships he captured on the high seas. Prominent people went to his refuge in Barataria where booty from ships plundered by the pirate bands was sold at discount prices. Luxury items brought the highest prices. To add insult to injury, the Creoles protected Lafitte from the new officials. Governor Claiborne offered $500 for the capture of the bold buccaneer. Lafitte countered with a $1,500 reward on the governor's head. This flamboyant figure in *The Buccaneer* becomes a hero when offering his services to General Andrew Jackson before the Battle of New Orleans. Jackson's ragtag militia and volunteers needed gunpowder and flints for their rifles. Although Jackson at first wrote off the Baratarians as "hellish banditti," according to reliable sources, Lafitte could have met with Andrew Jackson in a number of places in the Vieux Carré.

President James Madison and the Congress

declared war on Britain in 1812 in response to the practice by the British fleet of stopping U.S. ships to take men who were believed to be deserters. The U.S. Government perceived this as an illegal impressment of American sailors. When Emperor Napoleon went into exile on Elba after the defeat of his armies in 1814, the British unleashed experienced naval and land forces in raids against the United States on the Atlantic coast and in the Great Lakes. These forces burned the White House, the capitol, and many other buildings in Washington. President Madison and his cabinet fled after a battle at Blandensburg on the outskirts of Washington. After an unsuccessful bombardment of Fort McHenry by the British in Baltimore, the Americans began to strengthen defensive positions. The British command wanted to lessen the burden on the overextended forces fighting on the Canadian front by attacking New Orleans.

In the last week of November 1814, a large British expeditionary force set out from Jamaica, fought a naval battle on Lake Borgne with American gunboats, and proceeded to load troops off ships into shallow draft barges. The boats found a passage with the help from local fishermen through a canal to the banks of the Mississippi River. The advance forces made their way to the Villere Plantation by way of Bayou Bienvenue, only about 7 miles south of New Orleans. The city was in a panic when Jackson arrived.

Jackson (Charlton Heston) gets an amnesty for Lafitte (Yul Brynner) and his men when the pirate turns into a patriot. In reality, only Dominique You (Charles Boyer) and some other Baratarians in two gun groups fought from behind the Jackson Line, a six foot high earthen redoubt extending from the river to the cypress swamps on the Chalmette battlefield. In *The Buccaneer* Lafitte appears as a hero who measures the distance between the American fortifications and General Edward Packenham's British attacking forces. Lafitte did fulfill his promises but he was not present on the Chalmette Battlefield. Jackson assigned him to guard one of the strategic water routes to New Orleans.

The film, *The Buccaneer,* is historically correct in depicting General Jackson in an emaciated condition when he arrives to take command. He was suffering from bouts of fever associated with malaria. Despite this he managed to function as a fierce leader. He rallied the people to defend the city by whatever means possible in a famous statement: "By the Eternal, they shall not sleep on our soil." A crucial night raid on the British encampment kept the adversary off balance when they tried to rest after the arduous trek through the swamps to the Villere Plantation. General Edward Pakenham arrived on Christmas Day 1814. This was three days after the troops set up headquarters at Chalmette. Night raids against the British camp by the

Americans proved effective in causing chaos within the invading army's ranks.

Indians, free people of color, European Creole units, slaves, the U.S. militia, Baratarians, and volunteers from Tennessee and Kentucky made up the bulk of the fighters behind the Jackson Line, about 4,000 total. The British attacking the redoubt numbered 7,000 well-trained, seasoned veterans, many of whom fought in the Peninsular Wars against Napoleon.

On January 8, 1815, Pakenham's army marched toward the earthen rampart. As the redcoats emerged from the morning fog, grapeshot from the Kentucky long rifles cut them down. Pakenham was hit twice, dying on the field as be attempted to mount a second horse. General Gibbs leading the 2nd Brigade was also killed. The Americans also fired from eight cannon batteries.

The British unit whose task was to carry ladders and fascines (bundles of wood) to scale the fortifications were unable to reach the objective in time. British morale was broken as the troops witnessed the deaths of Pakenham and Gibbs. Chaos and retreat from the carnage added to the casualties and about 2,000 British were killed. There were only about twelve Americans casualties behind the Jackson Line. The battle scenes in the movie according to many historians give the audience an authentic depiction of the Jackson Line as a redoubt built with earth, supported with timber, and extending from the Mississippi River to the cypress swamps. A canal already on the sugarcane field provided an additional line of defense.

In the beginning of the film, Cecil B. DeMille points to a map to make the viewers realize how strategic the battle was to be for the westward expansion. The ploy romanticizing Jean Lafitte's part in the victory might be considered a sub-plot. It consists of the privateer's romantic affair with one of Claiborne's daughters. The movie in the credits lists Lyle Saxon's book, *Lafitte the Pirate*, as a source for the screenplay. A flair for dramatic diversions by Hollywood does not diminish its importance if one is able to recognize the difference between "real" and "reel."

Within two hours, the British retreated from the Chalmette Battlefield. A British brigade was swept downstream while attempting to land reinforcements at Chalmette. The battle had started and ended before they could make a landing. The retreat after Pakenham's death was so disorderly and swift that General John Lambert, the next in command, decided not to renew hostilities. Some badly wounded troops received medical assistance from the Americans, and others were taken to the Ursuline Convent which was converted into a hospital. Some dead soldiers were buried in shallow graves on the battlefield. Special treatment was given to the bodies of Generals

Pakenham and Gibbs. Their corpses were eviscerated, placed in barrels of rum, and shipped back to London.

Pakenham and Gibbs are immortalized in a monument in St. Paul's Cathedral in London on the right hand side of the main altar. On top are statues of the two in full regalia uniforms worn by them in the battle. The inscription on the monument reads: "Erected at the Public Expense to the Memory of Major General the Honorable Sir Edward Pakenham, K.B. and of Major General Samuel Gibbs, Who Fell Gloriously on the 8th of January 1815, while Leading the Troops to an Attack of the Enemy's Works in Front of New Orleans."

In *The Buccaneer,* Lafitte and Jackson become heroes. However, in the film Lafitte is nearly hanged at a party given by Governor Claiborne when he takes responsibility for the sinking of an American ship by a band of his men. Jackson convinces the mob at the celebration to allow Lafitte time to escape. The pirate's mysterious disappearance poses the question that has never been answered. What happened to him after the Battle of New Orleans? He casts a long shadow in local mythology. We do know his brother-in-arms, Dominique You, is buried in St. Louis #2 Cemetery.

Charlton Heston's role as Andrew Jackson makes the film stronger. The actor resembles Jackson in looks and possesses the same backwoods charisma attributed to the historic figure. The soon to be seventh President of the United States was treated like a god by euphoric residents in New Orleans. During a ceremony in the Place d'Armes, later Jackson Square, General Jean B. Plauché, a prominent Creole leader, placed his sword at Jackson's feet and kissed him on both cheeks! Others compared him to Napoleon who at that time enjoyed a great deal of popularity among the French in the city.

Claiborne and Americans hoped that the Creoles had been transformed into Americans. However, the rivalry between Creoles and Americans persisted. In 1836 the city split into three separate municipalities due to continued animosity between the two. The Vieux Carré became the First Municipality (Creole), Faubourg St. Mary the Second (American), and Faubourg Marigny the Third (Creole and new immigrants mainly from Germany and Ireland). This odd arrangement lasted until 1852.

The Battle of New Orleans remains one of the seminal turning points in American history. The United States ceased to be a pawn in European power politics. New Orleans entered an era of unparalleled prosperity as the premiere port in the nation. By 1836, the port was the top exporter of goods in the nation, even exceeding New York. The Golden Age lasted until the outbreak of the Civil War. According to the 1840 census, it was the fourth largest city in the country with a population of 102,000. In the chapter covering the film *Jezebel* there will be further information about this period. Three inventions put the Crescent City in the economic spotlight: the cotton gin, the steamboat, and a new method used to granulate sugar successfully for commercial purposes. The plantations from Natchez to New Orleans produced the cash crops of cotton and sugar. The advent of the steamboat provided an ideal mode to transport goods up and down the River.

The riches accumulated in and around New Orleans made it a cultural hub in theater, music, art, and dance. As previously mentioned, Francophones and Americans continued to compete. Both cultural groups built grand hotels, e.g. the St. Louis Hotel in the Vieux Carré and the St. Charles Hotel in Faubourg St. Mary, the American sector. Elegant stores selling clothing, jewelry, furniture and all kinds of luxury products could be found on both sides of Canal Street, the "neutral ground" separating Creoles and Americans.

People flocked to the city seeking fortunes and the glamorous lifestyles which made New Orleans the "Paris of America." Judah P. Benjamin, according to his biographers, came to this exciting place in 1828 with five dollars in his pocket and an intellectual creativity for success. He married a young woman from an old distinguished Creole family. Judah rose quickly in a place where men were admired for ambition and talent. He soon owned a plantation, established a lucrative law practice, and was elected to the U.S. Senate, becoming the first Jewish Senator in the nation. His first residence was in the French Quarter next to his Creole in-laws. As seen in **The Buccaneer**, the Creoles continued their prosperity in this "oldest neighborhood" in New Orleans.

St. Louis Hotel

CHAPTER 5

JEZEBEL IN THE FRENCH QUARTER – 1840 -1877

JEZEBEL (1938)

In *Jezebel,* Bette Davis creates the character of Julie, a high society, strong-willed Southern belle. It contains numerous scenes set in the French Quarter in the 1850s. It is commonly called the black and white *Gone With the Wind* because Julie and Scarlett represent strong-willed Southern belles. Davis wanted the role of Scarlett (along with 1,400 other actresses). Some observers of the competition for the part referred to it as "Scarlett fever." Antebellum New Orleans, as seen in the prior chapter, saw enormous growth in population and wealth during the Golden Era. The movie takes place in this period. Opening in theaters in 1938, a year before *Gone With the Wind,* this epic movie spared no expense to match the much anticipated glamour of Margaret Mitchell's Civil War story.

William Wyler directed the Warner Brothers extravaganza with an eye for perfection. The title of the screenplay comes from a figure in the Old Testament.

Aunt Belle Massey, played by Fay Bainter, at one point in the film denounces Julie as a "jezebel" or a conniving and shameful woman. Aunt Belle witnesses Julie's (Bette Davis) behavior in a scheme to cause a duel between her former beau and Preston Dillard (Henry Fonda), her former fiancé, who comes back to New Orleans with a wife from the North.

Both Davis and Bainter won Oscars as Best Actress and Best Supporting Actress for their performances in the movie. The film is a lesson in history. It is the beginning of a time, when railroads and the abolition of slavery threaten the monopoly in transportation by steamboats on the Mississippi River and the existence of plantation economies. These issues are discussed frequently by the actors in the film.

We are given valuable insights into the way people tried to fight the pestilence of yellow fever. In 1853, the worst "yellow jack" epidemic struck New Orleans. It is estimated that about 10,000 people died from the disease in a span of a few months. Books and other written accounts about the epidemic fall short of the visual account of the plight of the characters in the movie.

Several sequences in *Jezebel* try to show how the Vieux Carré appeared in the 1850s. The most ambitious and costly scenes are depictions of the legendary bar in the St. Louis Hotel, during its heyday as a landmark in the French Quarter. On your walking tour, you are able to view five original arches of this historic hotel. Research on the St. Louis Hotel tells us that the St. Louis Hotel (originally the City Exchange Hotel) was designed by the renowned architect, J.N.B. de Pouilly. It was a massive structure built in 1838 at a cost of $1.5 million. The huge dome of the building projected into the sky over the Vieux Carré. On the inside, the rotunda under the dome was lined with sixteen forty-feet high Corinthian columns. The rotunda sixty-six feet wide rose eighty-six feet under the dome with a fourteen-foot oculus.

The Corinthian columns were covered with stucco that was marbleized, had bases of iron and capitals of black cypress. The walls were covered with fresco paintings showing different cities in Europe and America painted by a pupil of the famous Italian artist, Dominique Canova. The circular grand staircase, public rooms, and ballroom are said to have been more beautiful and larger than any other in the United States. The dome with a copper top weighed about 100 tons. On either side of the rotunda there were auction blocks, one for slaves and another for luxury goods of all types. The St. Louis Hotel was the center for the Creole elite and the most magnificent building in the state. The majestic hotel was damaged by fire in 1840 but one million dollars was used to restore it to its former glory.

Aside from glittering balls and masquerades in social life, the hotel was the hub for business transactions. To keep merchants in the hotel for most of the day, it had a spacious reading room and a great bar that established the practice of serving complimentary food to the patrons. This food service at bars proved to be so popular that other bars throughout the city followed it as a model for attracting customers.

In *Jezebel,* well-dressed gentlemen are shown descending a staircase to a bar, decorated with mirrors and a long carved wooden bar on one side. The entire room is lit by ornate crystal chandeliers. This Hollywood set tried to imitate the most famous of the bars of that time in the Vieux Carré. In the film, food is set out at one end of the long bar, but the idea of a bar placed in a basement does not fit into the realities of a below sea-level topography. While Warner Brothers Studio may have put a lot of time and money into duplicating the bar, the final set is an invention of imagination by the set designers, but is nonetheless fairly authentic in its attempt to re-create the physical appearance of the St. Louis Hotel bar in the 1850s. In the present day, the Royal Orleans Hotel stands on the spot occupied by the old hotel, and there is an excellent painting of the exterior of the St. Louis Hotel in the lobby by A. Boyd Cruise.

The distinguished English writer, John Galsworthy, and his wife visited the crumbling hotel in 1915. Shortly after his tour of the structure, it was torn down by order from local health officials. His vivid description of the hotel, with photographs taken for an article in the local paper, gives us probably the last valuable source on the grandeur of early days of the building as it inspired the author, even in its ruined state. The bar was to the right of the rotunda as one entered the building from St. Louis Street, and it was on the ground floor, not underneath the lobby.

The site remained a parking lot until the Royal Orleans Hotel was built in 1960. The architect of the new hotel, Arthur Q. Davis, remembers how during construction all means possible had been used to copy the original building. Samuel Wilson, Jr., acting as a historical consultant on the project, stated: "Of course, we were greatly influenced by the style of the St. Louis Hotel. We gave the Royal Orleans the same height as the St. Louis had, a similar cornice line, a similar mass. The total exterior impact of the Royal Orleans is the same as that of the St. Louis."

Davis tells us about the five arches as the last remnants of the original building. When clearing the site, the arches, which served as a model for all the new arches, were taken down piece by piece, numbered and put into storage. On the Chartres Street side where the five old arches stood, the pieces in the construction stage were carefully put back with precision on the same spot where they stood. If you gaze at the five arches, you will see that even the aged lettering in the plaster are still visible.

It is indeed fortunate for one to be able to reflect upon how this piece of Vieux Carré history would have appeared in the 19th century. The appearance on screen of scenes in the bar in *Jezebel* prompts us to imagine how the hotel might have appeared in those days. In this respect, with a little work we can use the film as a starting point to appreciate the historical importance attributed to the original structure (see the sketch of the St. Louis Hotel).

Turning our attention to the movie's episodes on the 1853 yellow fever epidemic, we watch Preston Dillard (Henry Fonda) as he collapses in the St. Louis bar from the effects of "yellow jack." On screen, the panic gripping New Orleans is true to historical accounts. Quarantine lines around the city and the problems dealing with the sick and dead are revealed in the movie. The firing of cannons into the sky and burning barrels filled with tar is of historical significance because the prevailing belief at that time was "evil vapors" or a miasma carried by the winds from the swamps surrounding New Orleans was the principal cause of yellow fever epidemics. It was said at the time that these gases came from putrid and decaying substances so common in the swamps. The solution to this involved dispelling these fumes from the air over the city with cannon fire and burning tar.

The mosquito *aedes egypti* was the airborne carrier but this was not proven until the early 1900s after the Spanish-American War. The theory of miasma was correct in identifying the summer or warm months as periods when the fever was known to occur and was transmitted in the air. People who could afford to leave the city during the summers went to the Gulf Coast or other places away from the swamps. Mosquito netting over beds allowed people to sleep without being attacked by swarms of insects.

At one point in the film, Preston swats a mosquito from his neck and later falls victim to yellow fever at the St. Louis Hotel bar. The other patrons in the bar move away from him and cover their mouths with handkerchiefs. He is carried to Julie's house in town. The front door is marked with a large "Y" to warn others that a fever victim is in the house. In many respects the movie captures the public fear of the disease. The isolation of the victims and the establishment of quarantine lines correctly portrays practices in those days. Also, once a person was infected with yellow fever, medical treatment became a waiting game. Damp cloths were applied to the patient until he or she died, or survived the fever.

In *Jezebel*, Julie (Bette Davis) manages to cross a quarantine line into town from her plantation to be at Preston's bedside. This is a mission to redeem herself from being labeled a conniving and self-centered "jezebel." When Preston's wife arrives, Julie begs her to be allowed to accompany Preston to an island on the outskirts of the city, where victims are being taken for further care. Redemption is a central theme at the end of the film. It is high drama because she is risking her own life to save his. One argument she uses to convince his wife is that as a native she is better able to communicate with others at the hospital where the patients are being transported.

When she boards a wagon with him as it rolls through the city, the footage on screen shows the tar barrels burning and cannons blasting. Symbols of heroism during the epidemics were the Sisters of Charity. These nuns are shown comforting victims on the wagon caravan rolling out of the city. Their presence adds a new dimension to Julie's transformation into a heroine by risking her life while trying to save Pres.

As mentioned previously, *Jezebel* as a title for the film is traced to a remark made by Julie's Aunt Belle branding her as a "jezebel" described in the Bible. One incident reaffirming the label is Julie choosing a red dress to wear to the Olympus Ball. In the movie, the ball is not described as a Mardi Gras ball, but it is a formal dance where unmarried women are expected to wear white gowns (the film shows us a mock king on a platform). This tradition still exists at the Rex Ball on Mardi Gras night, when debutantes are presented to the King and Queen. In *Jezebel*, Julie decides to wear a red dress in defiance of all the rules established by social clubs which present debutantes to the members of high society.

Preston escorts Julie to the Olympus Ball and glares at anyone who might pass a remark about the scandalous red dress. When she picks out the gown at the shop of a dressmaker, several of her friends and family members show disapproval by stating: "Only a woman from Gallatin Street would wear a red dress!" Gallatin Street in French Quarter history was an infamous section where prostitutes plied their trade.

From a historical perspective, it is worth noting that the legendary red dress would have been a shocking display in social circles. Julie's family could be expected to express their feelings about this affront, but once she is in the company of Pres at the Ball, he would adhere to what was known in Creole times as the *Code Duello*. Any gentleman who showed open disapproval of her choice of a dress would be challenged to a duel by Pres to defend her honor. At the time, there were a number of fencing schools on what is now Exchange Alley where men like Pres could learn the skills necessary to adhere to the *Code Duello*. In other cases, pistols rather than swords were used in duels. The places used for duels included the "duelling oaks" at Allard Plantation, now City Park. Under live oak trees, with Spanish moss festooning down from their limbs duelists settled affairs of honor early in the morning. According to historical records, Don José Pepe Llulla was the most well-known duelist in New Orleans history. In forty-one matches he was never defeated. He also owned St. Vincent De Paul Cemetery, located downriver from the Vieux Carré.

In *Jezebel*, when Ted Dillard kills Buck Cantrell in a duel with pistols in the film, it takes place early in the morning and involves a code of honor ritualized in 1850s New Orleans. If any man at the Olympus Ball would have disagreed with Preston's remarks even about the weather, he would take this as an affront to Julie who was wearing a red dress. The emotional tension in that scene in the film shows how deep the duelling code is instilled in a man's belief system. Pres was ready to defend his fiancée's honor in a duel to the death. One of the characters in the picture, Dr. Livingston, describes a woman in high society as "a frail, delicate chalice to be cherished and protected." The movie is based upon a play by Owen Davis, Sr., which was purchased by Warner Brothers. The film was a box-office hit in 1938 and is often featured on the Turner Classic Movie television channel.

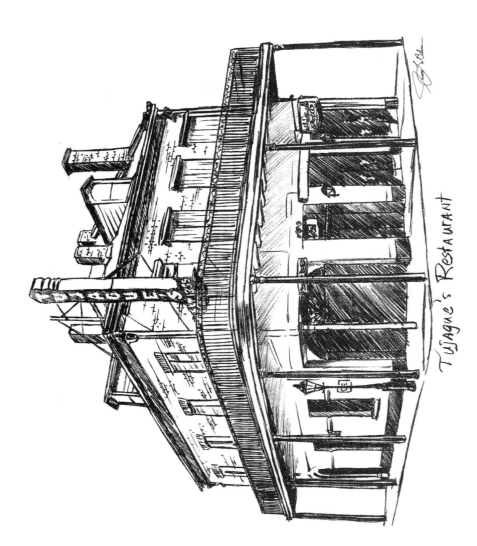

Tujague's Restaurant

CHAPTER 6

CLIO DULAINE IN POSTBELLUM NEW ORLEANS

SARATOGA TRUNK (1945)

In the opening scene of the film *Saratoga Trunk*, Clio Dulaine (Ingrid Bergman), Angèlique (Flora Robson), her maid, and Cupidon (Jerry Austin), her dwarf man servant, stare at 1870s New Orleans from the deck of a ship as it begins to dock at the wharves on the Mississippi River. Immediately, we are reminded that the port city was the entry point for so many immigrants and settlers coming to the New World. In the movie, the spires of St. Louis Cathedral rise high over the landscape.

Clio, Angèlique, and Cupidon lived in Paris with Rita Dulaine, Clio's mother. Rita, a mistress, was sent into exile by the aristocratic Creole family of Dulaine after Nicolas Dulaine (Clio's father) died of a bullet wound while grabbing a pistol from Rita as she attempted to commit suicide. Clio (Bergman), now a stunningly beautiful and headstrong young woman, wants to avenge her mother's banishment and bury her body in the elite St. Louis Cemetery in New Orleans.

Her deceased mother, Rita Dulaine, owned a house on Rampart Street, wore gowns and jewels from Paris, and took trips to Europe with Nicolas Dulaine. As the only son in a wealthy family, Nicolas followed the rules of the unique Creole arrangement named *plaçage*, or placement, of a free woman of color into an arrangement that gave her money, property, and rights for any children born from the union. Rita was a *placée* who gave birth to Clio. She was the gorgeous mistress of Nicolas and enjoyed the luxuries he gave her. When he married a European woman, Rita's world was shattered. Now there were two Dulaine families in New Orleans. In Edna Ferber's novel, ***Saratoga Trunk***, upon which the movie is based, Rita's situation is described: "Love, luxury, adulation, even position of a sort, Rita Dulaine had everything that a beautiful and beloved woman can have except the security of a legal name and a legal right as consort of Nicolas Dulaine."

Ingrid Bergman, as Clio, displays a wide range of talent. It is a must see picture for Bergman fans. No character in any movie examined in this book gives us a greater sense of history in New Orleans than Clio Dulaine in ***Saratoga Trunk***. Set in the post Civil War period in the Vieux Carré, it takes the moviegoer on a trip through the French Quarter that is full of images of the past and important to the present day. Bergman's role as Clio is not very often recognized as a highlight in her career. In 1942, she won great accolades for her role in the film **Casablanca,** a movie which is on almost everyone's list as one of the greatest, if not the greatest, film ever made in Hollywood. In **Saratoga Trunk** as Clio Dulaine, as we have already seen, she is the daughter of a free woman of color and a European Creole father who comes back to the city from Paris to claim her rights as a child from a *plaçage* union between her parents. Since early childhood in Paris, Clio has been told stories about the charm and allure of New Orleans. Now as a young woman with familial roots in the city, she is a visitor. Through her eyes we are able to see what makes the Vieux Carré a place of unique appeal.

From all accounts, Ingrid Bergman was delighted to be in the role of what she called "a New Orleans bitch" after such demanding assignments in **Casablanca** and **For Whom the Bell Tolls.** The film was shot during the dark days of World War II but not released into theaters until 1945.

This was a low budget production made into a movie without any location filming in the Vieux Carré. Some critics find fault with the artificiality of the sets in Hollywood, but those who are familiar with the French Quarter praise the recreations of widely known buildings and places. The movie brings to life the Old French Market, the St. Louis Cathedral, the French Opera House, and numerous street scenes in the Quarter during the 1870s (see sketches of some of these places).

At this point, it is worthwhile to highlight some of the most notable scenes in the film. Clio Dulaine, accompanied by her maid and butler, reopens her mother's house on Rampart Street. The next morning, her servants walk with her through the streets to the Old French Market. She sashays through the food and vegetable stalls. Along the way, she sees black children playing in an informal "spasm" or street band, predating jazz, and street vendors singing about their baskets of berries. Then she smells jambalaya! In her finest Parisian attire, she stops to taste a dish of jambalaya at one of the food stands. Calling herself "Madame la Comtesse," she becomes the center of attention for all the merchants and shoppers. They stare at her and eagerly await her opinion about the dish. The people in the market are thrilled when she declares, "Oh, it's delicious, it's better than anything I've eaten in France."

Gary Cooper (Clint Maroon), a well-dressed cowboy from Texas, admires her beauty and persona. He offers her a ride in his coach to Madame Begué's Restaurant for brunch. But before she is able to accept, she is whisked off to another carriage by her maid Angèlique, played by the renowned British actress Flora Robson, who wears black face makeup and a multi-colored headdress for the part.

The stark contrast between the beautiful Gallic lady and the man from Texas reflected the negative view of well-bred New Orleans Creoles toward their neighbors to the West. This stereotypical view of cowboys is accentuated when Clio, the *femme fatale* from Paris, is seen next to Clint. It was so upsetting to Angèlique that she referred to him as "that Texan" because she is accustomed to the elite social circles in Paris within which Rita and her relatives moved while Clio was still a child. Certainly, in Angèlique's mind, the long ocean voyage to New Orleans could not end in a liaison between the lovely and cultured young woman under her protection and a "cowboy." Angèlique knew the ways of the world more than her mistress and was determined to prevent her from disgrace by being in the company of a man from the Wild West.

Clio vows to take revenge against a system that relegated her mother to the odd world in which she remained a *placée.* Early in the film, when Clio is in her mother's house in New Orleans, she throws open the louvered shutters and shouts: "I'll show them, these pasty-faced aristocrats! They will find out there is someone on Rampart Street who is not afraid of them. Everything they did to Mama, I'll do it back to them." The Vieux Carré was the place where Clio could relive her mother's happiest times. In this quest, she could also go to all the places frequented by the other Dulaine family, such as St. Louis Cathedral,

Madame Begué's Restaurant, the French Opera House and other gathering spots for Creole aristocracy. In the film, she takes the audience to all these sites. In doing so, she gives moviegoers a glimpse of what the Vieux Carré was like in the 1870s.

Clio Dulaine guides us through a city that regained its position as the center of culture and entertainment after the Civil War. It is not a coincidence that Rhett and Scarlett came to New Orleans for a honeymoon in *Gone With the Wind*.

As pointed out earlier, *Saratoga Trunk* was made at a Hollywood studio and is a movie whose artistic effectiveness paints a realistic picture of the post Civil War Vieux Carré. One could argue that a facsimile of life of the French Quarter in the era was created on studio sets. People who lived in the Quarter in the 1940s when the movie was made will tell you that this section of the city had seen better days but still had the charm of the late 19th Century. It was full of dilapidated buildings even though the Vieux Carré Commission and the preservation movement managed to keep a status quo. The French Opera House burned down in 1919, Madame Begué's became Tujaque's Restaurant, but the Cathedral of the 1850's is still the heart of the French Quarter.

In this respect, the film is a celluloid record of what may have existed in the French Quarter in the

1870s. In a darkened theater or at home watching a video, we are mesmerized by a vanished environment that is vividly described in books. These images are of historical value because they take us back in time with a certain degree of authenticity. The movie was shot on Hollywood sets in the 1940s. Taking this into account, the art director's ideas about New Orleans in the 1870s define how the place looked. It must be stressed that despite the limitations in the sets, the picture gives filmgoers an important view of Creole life in that time period.

The most intriguing moments in the movie can be traced to Edna Ferber's novel. Reading the book and watching the movie, or vice versa, lends support to the argument that films are artistic contributions to popular culture in a society that is oriented toward visual productions. If you see the movie and miss some of the messages conveyed, you can go to the book to clear up questions about the story because the script closely follows the novel. Many cinema fans will often view their favorite movies multiple times, and learn something more which they might have missed when watching it at another time.

One very clever ploy used in the story is her relationship with Clint Maroon who, while coming from a completely different background, shares her passion for addressing the injustices found in both of their lives. She takes on New Orleans Creole society and he attacks the American railroad establishment. Both have suffered from two powerful and vicious systems.

Several scenes in the movie are captivating. One takes place at Madame Begué's Restaurant. Clio and her servants sit at a table usually reserved by the Dulaine family. Clio speaks to Hippolyte Begué in her best Parisian French. He is in awe of her aristocratic manners, as she mentions that Begué's is well-known in Paris for its cuisine. After she begins eating, the women of the other Dulaine family come to the entrance and are shocked to see Rita Dulaine's daughter at their table. They make a quick exit. Then Clint Maroon comes into the restaurant. Seated at a table across the room, he is having difficulty ordering from a menu in French. He calls the waiter "cookee," a term commonly used for cooks on cattle drives in the West.

Clio notices him, and signals the head waiter to ask Clint if he would like to join her. Much to Angèlique's displeasure, he comes over to the table. Clio again, in Parisian French, orders the house specialty, kidney stew in a special sauce prepared by Hippolyte Begué himself. When the dish arrives, Clint asks Monsieur Begué if he has ketchup to put on it. The owner can hardly believe his ears, but Clio tells him that ketchup is used widely in Paris. After this Wild West-meets-cultural New Orleans encounter, Clio and Clint laugh loudly about the incident and the expression on the owner's face when they are leaving Begué's in Clint's carriage.

After embarrassing the Creole Dulaines at the restaurant, Clio goes to all the places where she might see them again, the French Opera House, St. Louis Cathedral, and rides past their home in the Vieux Carré. Finally, a lawyer comes to Clio's house on Rampart Street to offer her a sum of money from the Dulaine family to leave New Orleans. She and the lawyer agree to a figure in dollars. Then Clio makes a demand that her mother's body be buried in St. Louis Cemetery #I with the stipulation that every year on All Saints' Day, fresh flowers are to be placed on the grave and insists the inscription on the grave read "Rita Dulaine."

As the lawyer is leaving Clio's house, a camera zooms in on her face for a close-up. He stutters, saying, "You are very beautiful - that is beautiful." She replies: "Yes, isn't it lucky?" This confirms the opinion expressed by historians about the striking loveliness of women of color in New Orleans. While examining this phenomenon in *The Feast of All Saints*, we saw that European Creole women envied the Creole of color women for their beauty.

Saratoga Trunk is remarkable for many reasons. The stars, Ingrid Bergman and Gary Cooper, glisten on the screen with a romantic chemistry which existed between them in the 1943 film *For Whom the Bell Tolls* based on Ernest Hemingway's movie. Flora Robson who plays Angèlique was nominated for an Oscar for Best Supporting Actress. The musical score by Max Steiner is superb. He also wrote the scores for *Jezebel*, *Gone With the Wind*, and *Casablanca* during the Golden Age of Hollywood in the 1930s and 1940s. For native New Orleanians there is a special appeal because the story covers a lot of tales about the Vieux Carré handed down from previous generations, and recorded in writings on the history of the French Quarter.

When we first see the film, so many parts in the dialogue and scenes strike us as useful in attempting to understand life in the Vieux Carré in the 1870s. At one time, two-thirds of the property in the French Quarter was owned by free women of color especially in the vicinity of Rampart Street. This goes back to the time when the system named *plaçage* gave these women property and income for life, even if the arrangement between the man and woman ended. Another piece in local folklore contends that Creole society, in an attempt to preserve a way of life, continued to focus on Paris as the "mother city" that set the trends in fashion, food and culture. Thus we see Monsieur Begué's joy in hearing from Clio that people in the French capitol talk about his famous brunch, a late breakfast believed to have originated at Beguès.

In real history, at one time Madame Begué's husband was a butcher who brought meat to the French Market early in the morning before refrigeration was invented. Afterwards, he and his fellow butchers came to the restaurant for a late breakfast when they finished work at the meat market across the street from Begué's. Today in New Orleans, jazz brunches are very popular and are thought to have originated as the hearty meals served at Begue's. The restaurant at the Royal Sonesta Hotel is called Begué's to honor the cuisine served at that legendary place. Today, Tujaque's Restaurant on Decatur is on the original site of Madame Begué's.

In the movie, as Clio is dusting the chandelier in a room of the Rampart Street house, she quotes an old Louisiana proverb from her mother: "Give a Creole a crystal chandelier and two mirrors,"

Angèlique responds to Clio: "Who's Creole here? Your mama was a *placée!* Take shame on yourself, denying your own mama," (The term *placée* is defined in Chapter 3.)

The street vendors, chimney sweepers, and spasm bands were important in the folkways in Creole society and are shown in the film. Their songs and music set the rhythm in the Quarter each day. The men peddling coal chant the melody, "Mah mule is white, Mah face is black; Ah sells mah coal, Two bits a sack." Clio sings a song at the piano in the African-French patois. When Clint asks her the name of the language, she replies, "Gombo." Angèlique at one point speaks about *gris-gris* used in Voodoo to cast a spell of evil or luck. Many other unique Louisiana customs appear in the movie.

Columns Hotel

CHAPTER 7

THE LEGACY OF STORYVILLE – 1897-1917

NEW ORLEANS (1947) AND PRETTY BABY (1978)

New Orleans' heritage is revealed in many films. What is seen depends upon the knowledge and life experience of individual viewers. If one is curious about a particular historical period, event, place, or character making up this legacy, that person might draw upon different sources to gain more knowledge about a subject. Al Rose, author of **Storyville, New Orleans,** tells readers how he became interested in a place of the past which adults talked about during his childhood with a certain tone of yearning as "the District."

Rose was born in New Orleans one year before Storyville was shut down by the United States Department of the Navy. In subsequent years, his inquisitive interest in Storyville and its role in jazz history led him to engage in years of research. His book includes many rare photographs which take the reader on a visual trip through America's best-known red-light district. Rose's book's subtitle is: **Being an**

***Authentic, Illustrated Account of the Notorious
Red-light District.***

In 1897, Alderman Sidney Story, in an attempt
to exercise control over the spread of prostitution in
New Orleans put forward an ordinance to confine
it to a thirty-eight block section fronting on Basin
Street outside but adjacent to the legal boundaries
of the Vieux Carré. When the ordinance passed into
municipal law, the cultured alderman did not dream
that "the District" would be named after him and
would flourish for twenty years. Jazz was not invented
in Storyville, but about two hundred musicians playing
it started their careers there. Jelly Roll Morton and
King Oliver are among the jazz greats who played in
Storyville.

Lulu White and Josie Arlington were two of
the most famous madames who became wealthy
by operating brothels in the red-light district. Tom
Anderson was the de facto mayor of Storyville.
The ***Blue Book*** listed the prostitutes and contained
advertisements for bars, liquor, beer, restaurants, and
gambling.

Two movies attempting to depict Storyville are
New Orleans and ***Pretty Baby. New Orleans*** features
Louis Armstrong and Billie Holiday. Its fictional
account of the emergence of jazz nationwide after the
closing down of Storyville is not completely accurate.

But the film is important for two reasons. First, Louis Armstrong's band demonstrates why jazz became a national obsession. Second, this is the only movie in which Billie Holiday, the most famous of blues singers, appears. She sings "Do You Know What It Means To Miss New Orleans?" In the film *New Orleans*, Kid Ory, Barney Bigard, and other early jazz artists play in the band with Louis Armstrong. In keeping with the history of jazz, the film does follow this American music form from New Orleans to Chicago. After the demise of Storyville, many of the best jazz musicians played on excursion boats running up and down the Mississippi and then moved to places like Chicago and New York where they could make a better living as musicians.

All that remains of "the District" on the map in this book is a part of Lulu White's Annex on the corner of Basin and Bienville Streets. The one-story orange brick building is now the Basin Street Super Market (a grocery store adjacent to the Iberville public housing project). The ornate Victorian mansions serving as brothels or "sporting houses" were torn down and replaced with this housing project. Basin Street became famous in music and song, e.g. "Basin Street Blues." The origin of the name "basin" comes from the turning basin at the end of the Carondelet Canal which extended from Bayou St. John to this area near the French Quarter.

In this section, on the outskirts of the Vieux Carré, there was an area where slaves gathered on Sundays to practice and enjoy dances and rituals (including the bamboula and voodoo) brought with them from Africa and the West Indies. It was named Congo Square. Over the years, Congo Square became important for preserving African heritage. Today Congo Square is part of Armstrong Park. In the center of the park's greenspace there is a statue of Louis Armstrong. The internationally acclaimed musician is New Orleans' best-known native son. It is very fitting that Louis Armstrong be honored with a monument and park near Basin Street, where he got his start as a jazz great, when he learned his art from some of the musicians who played in Storyville. Also, Louis Armstrong International Airport and the Satchmo Summer Fest are tributes to this jazz legend.

The Carondelet Canal existed from 1795 until about 1930. Although it lay outside the Vieux Carré, it figured heavily into keeping the flow of trade into the Old City. The turning basin area was famous for bars, gambling, and womanizing. It was here that prostitutes set up their own trade around the time of the Battle of New Orleans as they saw the profits to be made from the men who came from American territories to fight in the war. The same loose women catered to the many flatboat men who brought goods down the river from regions like Kentucky and Tennessee prior to the

Louisiana Purchase.

The problem of "lewd women" was present during the colonial periods and can be traced back to the sending "correction girls" from France to provide female companions for the early settlers. Indeed, the procurement of women for the colony came naturally to the French governments who saw prostitution as a natural part of society. The colonial officials did attempt to keep these women outside the boundaries of the Vieux Carré in the back of town. By the 1850s a new habitat for the prostitutes came into being in the Gallatin Street section downriver from the French Market. The Storyville experiment later tried to confine brothels in a specific area.

Al Rose in his book mentions the film *New Orleans* released in 1947 as a work that glosses over the truth about the closing of Storyville in 1917 by putting the spotlight on the famous figures Louis Armstrong and Billie Holiday as a glamorous diversion. Now we should take a look at the controversial movie *Pretty Baby*. The screenplay writers in the credits claim to have used Rose's book as a primary source for the story.

In *Pretty Baby*, director Louis Malle takes on difficult social issues arising from the twenty raucous years when Storyville existed. The most sensitive subject is putting virgins up for bid to patrons at brothels.

Brooke Shields plays Violet, a 12-year-old girl raised in a palatial sporting house by a resident prostitute mother "Hattie," played by Susan Sarandon. Violet is auctioned off on her 12th birthday as a ceremony to introduce her to a life as a prostitute, by selling her virginity to a house patron who offers the highest bid. She is paraded around on a litter to be examined by men in attendance for the event. The scene is morally and emotionally repugnant to many moviegoers, but is in keeping with the reality of Storyville.

Even though the movie was rated "R," some film critics denounced it as shocking. Chronicles of Storyville reveal that the sale of virgins took place many times in "the District." The makers of the movie, in some circles, were praised for writing a sensitive script that tried to soften the lurid aspects in the film by stressing beauty in cinematography and the importance of human relationships in coping with life in a brothel.

In Hollywood, Susan Sarandon was able to excel as an actress in other roles, most notably in *Dead Man Walking* (1995) a part for which she won a Best Actress Oscar. That movie was based upon a true Louisiana story about a nun who championed the rights of a man on death row. Many film critics believe Brooke Shields does a remarkable job in her role as Violet. However, after *Pretty Baby* she appeared in several second-rate motion pictures. Shields is more widely-known for modeling and commercials and not as a film actress.

Ernest J. Bellocq, a real historical figure in New Orleans, is played by Keith Carradine. He was a pioneer in photography, credited with taking pictures of prostitutes which are now considered works of art. He also photographed the interiors and exteriors of houses in Storyville. These pictures serve as scarce records available to researchers. The houses ranged from wealthy, opulent structures to crude one room cribs. Mahogany Hall and Josie Arlington's house were huge Victorian style buildings decorated with fine crystal chandeliers, luxurious furniture, and contained elegant staircases. Large rooms used as dance halls and bars provided customers with bands that played until daylight.

All of the great houses were demolished. When the film was made in New Orleans, the Columns Hotel (see a sketch of the hotel) on St. Charles Avenue was the site for interior footage because it presents the grandiose features found in the legendary palaces on Basin Street. Exterior shots used smaller houses in the Lower Garden District on streets near St. Charles Ave., e.g. 1221 Orange Street.

The pictures *New Orleans* and *Pretty Baby* reproduce an important time in New Orleans history. On the St. Charles Avenue streetcar tour, we see the Columns Hotel (See a sketch of the Columns Hotel).

Anyone who goes into this hotel will recognize the interior from *Pretty Baby*. We can visualize the jazz legend, Jelly Roll Morton, playing for patrons in a Storyville brothel. Antonio Fargas, playing the character of Professor in the film, gives a terrific performance as the brothel's piano player. It is clear that this actor represents Jelly Roll Morton with the important role. Fargas has been praised for his onscreen talent as an actor and musician.

For a view of what Storyville looked like before it was closed down in 1917, photographs by Ernest J. Bellocq give historians a visual record of the place. In the film, Bellocq, played by Keith Carradine, is shown as a handsome leading man. Al Rose tells us in his book, *Storyville, New Orleans*, that Bellocq was a short man with a squeaky voice and a thick French accent who was a respected figure in the District. The prostitutes whom he photographed seemed to like him because he showed sensibility toward his photographic subjects.

Both *New Orleans* and *Pretty Baby* show how Storyville on the screen can be transformed from historic reality into folklore. The theme of "fallen women" plays well to movie audiences. And when prostitution is romanticized in stories about New Orleans, it becomes a legacy of the city.

French Quarter Courtyard

CHAPTER 8

THE FILMS OF THE GREAT DEPRESSION ERA – 1928-1940S

THE CINCINNATI KID (1965) AND WALK ON THE WILD SIDE (1962)

As a port city and railroad terminus, New Orleans in the Great Depression attracted hustlers, drifters, and hoboes with meager hopes for finding jobs. The lure to a city that had the reputation of violating conventional rules brought many people seeking quick money. They were willing to live on the edge of the law in a place known for a laissez faire attitude to authority. Some who rode the rails might find employment in transitory or menial jobs requiring little or no skills. The Vieux Carré tolerated shady characters who could move freely within the slum areas in this section especially near the docks.

Two films in the book take place in this era: *The Cincinnati Kid* and **Walk on the Wild Side.** One is the story about a wandering card-shark, and the other is about a woman living in the comfort of a cat house. In each case, the main figures in the plots lead transitory ways of life.

In ***The Cincinnati Kid***, Steve McQueen plays Eric, an up and coming card-shark, who wants to challenge Lancey (Edward G. Robinson) in poker to establish him as "the Man" in gaming circles nationwide. A showdown stud poker game brings to New Orleans the big name card-sharks of the Depression era. Using vintage cars and the French Quarter for the movie is a big plus toward capturing what things may have been like during the Great Depression.

Even though the movie was released as late as 1965, the city's skyline did not have tall buildings. Towering office and hotel buildings rose during the oil boom in the late 1970s. These factors give the movie a 1930s appearance. Another positive in the decision to shoot on location in the Quarter is to capture its identity with hedonism.

When director Norman Jewison replaced Sam Peckinpah, who was fired by the producer (Martin Ransohoff), he insisted upon using the Vieux Carré for many scenes. The studio was concerned about going over budget. Jewison saw the project as a personal challenge. Originally, the picture was in black and white. The new director used color because he believed it would look more artistic on the screen, especially for the card game scenes which are key to the plot. From his perspective, only certain screenplays lent themselves fully to film noir. And this was long before poker became a spectator sport as seen on television with the World Poker Tour.

The film opens with Steve McQueen walking along a sidewalk next to a brick wall. As he reaches an opening in the wall, he is blocked by a funeral procession entering the cemetery accompanied by the Eureka Brass Band. It is a jazz funeral, identified with the only city in the United States where this ritual takes place. Hollywood sometimes gives the impression that jazz funerals take place on a daily basis. The truth is such rites are reserved to honor jazz musicians and occur infrequently. At the very start, there is no doubt about New Orleans as the location.

The Eureka Brass Band leads the funeral procession into St. Louis Cemetery #2 off of Basin Street. A shoe shine boy challenges McQueen to a game tossing coins against the wall after he makes his way through the crowd in the funeral parade. This challenge defines the theme in the movie as one stressing games of chance. McQueen's coin falls closest to the wall making him the winner. He says to the young boy, "I guess you are not ready for me yet, kid."

As the credits roll across the screen, the jazz procession marches through the streets to an upbeat tune. This indicates the deceased individual has been "cut loose" and delivered to a better place, presumably heaven. The people following the band strut and dance while some hold open umbrellas. In the jazz world this is known as "the second line." This is an effective way to introduce New Orleans to audiences in a movie theater.

After the Kid (Eric) takes part in a small poker game, which he wins, he gets into a fight with a player who accuses him of marking the cards. In a sequence after he escapes this fight he is pictured with Shooter (Karl Malden) on a ferry boat on the Mississippi River. From this vantage point you can see the large number of wharves lining the shores of this mighty waterway. The St. Louis Cathedral, the structure most often associated with the city, comes into view.

Edward G. Robinson, who plays the role of Lancey "the Man" Howard, disembarks from a train and takes a cab to a hotel. His presence in the city is spread by word to everyone who plays poker. Lancey has the reputation as the most successful and reigning champion stud poker player in national gaming circles.

Lancey takes on and soundly defeats William Jefferson Slade (Rip Torn) identified by Shooter as "coming from one of the richest families in the state." In the plot, Shooter, who has earned a reputation as an honest dealer, arranges for a showdown between Eric and Lancey in a high stakes poker game which will decide which one is entitled to be known as the stud poker champion.

It is worth noting that Lancey's skill at the card

table may be characterized as a skilled artist at work. Many experienced poker players from all over come to New Orleans to attend the showdown game between Lancey and Eric. It takes place at the Old Lafayette Hotel on St. Charles Avenue for several nights. In the crowded room there are many onlookers and players, including Lady Fingers (Joan Blondell) and Yeller (Cab Calloway).

An element making New Orleans the ideal setting for the story is the presence of old buildings and narrow streets in the Vieux Carré. By bringing in vintage cars and dressing the cast in period clothing, filmmakers created the atmosphere of the Great Depression. According to history, gambling has always been a passion for the local population. To underscore this, the film shows a cock fight attended by gambling spectators. Eric and many others wage bets on the fighting roosters as the birds battle to the death in a pit surrounded by bleachers of fans. In the "City That Care Forgot" some observers believe the tolerance of all sorts of vices might have developed from the fact that the place is primarily a port city more akin to Marseilles than any other place in the nation.

The colonial past with its love of gambling continued in New Orleans. We saw this in previous chapters. The early riverboat men who came to the port were attracted to all kinds of vices including gambling. A section in the introduction of *The WPA*

Guide To New Orleans, and attributed to Colonel Creecy, a visitor to the city, best describes the nature of lawlessness in New Orleans:

> "Negroes in purple and fine linen, and slaves in rags and chains. Ships, arks, steamboats, robbers, pirates, alligators, Assassins, gamblers, drunkards, and cotton speculators; Sailors, soldiers, pretty girls, and ugly fortune-tellers; Pimps, imps, shrimps, and all sorts of dirty fellows......"

This guide was originally published in 1938. Walker Percy, a well-known local writer, in his review of the 1983 revised edition of *The WPA Guide to New Orleans* declares it "still the best" and quotes a phrase from the above passage. When Colonel Creecy describes New Orleans as a meeting spot for "the pimps, the imps, and the shrimps," he adds that the city is characterized by a "liberal attitude toward human frailties." His depiction of New Orleans is appropriate for many of the movies covered in this book! Some places got rid of their eccentrics, some places tolerate them, in New Orleans they are often celebrated.

Given the fact that the writers of the 1938 edition of *The WPA Guide* put so much emphasis on New Orleans as a city whose nature stems from its role as a port, it follows that films would utilize techniques aimed at transporting spectators back in time to another important period in history.

The camera in 1965 in New Orleans as it pans across the skyline of the city from the Mississippi River in two scenes from ferries in *The Cincinnati Kid* is able to replicate the Depression era in the city. When the film was being shot, the Hibernia Bank Building was still the tallest building in town. In the 1930s the same building was the highest in the urban skyline. In the 1970s and 1980s, during the oil boom days, the skyline changed dramatically when buildings twice the height of the Hibernia Bank were built.

The moviegoer sees The French Quarter in the Depression as Eric soul-searches when roaming in this part of the city. While walking in the rain through Jackson Square and the French Quarter, he is approached by a prostitute. He ignores her perhaps to assure himself that he has not lost every shred of decency during his life as a drifter and gambler. He then strolls over to Preservation Hall (726 St. Peter St.) where the legendary piano player and singer, Sweet Emma Barrett, is singing a song about lost love in time with a jazz ensemble. By the time the movie was made in 1965, Preservation Hall had been open a few years and had become world-famous.

In a subplot, Eric pursues Christian (Tuesday Weld), even to the point of visiting her uninvited at her home on a farm. Christian and Shooter's wife, Melba

(Ann-Margaret), are friends who walk in the French Quarter shopping and go to a Turkish bath. Eric is not ready to marry and settle down with a job and family. When Christian finds her friend Melba in Eric's hotel room during a break in the big game, she sees him for what he is, i.e. a card-shark who is caught up in a fast life of gambling and testing his luck to the limit.

Another movie falling within the Depression years is **Walk on the Wild Side,** loosely based on a novel of the same name by Nelson Algren. It features top actors and actresses Laurence Harvey, Capucine, Barbara Stanwyck and Anne Baxter. This movie makes maximum use of the French Quarter and its landmarks (e.g. Jackson Square and St. Louis Cathedral). It is also Jane Fonda's debut on the big screen as a major player. The plot revolves around Dove Linkhorn's (Laurence Harvey) search for Hallie (Capucine) his former girlfriend whom he finds in the Doll House.

During his search for her, he hitchhikes and rides the rails from Texas. The address given in the film for the brothel catering to upper-class patrons is 904 Chartres near Jackson Square (see the route for the French Quarter Tour). The movie uses many locales in the Vieux Carré. One of the best features of the movie is the excellent musical score by Elmer Bernstein and Mack David. It was nominated for an Oscar in 1963 under the category "Best Music, Original Song."

The music by Bernstein is so engrossing that it almost overshadows the plot. During the opening credits, a black cat and a white cat fight after slinking around garbage cans and through pipes accompanied by the musical score. This sequence is remarkable in reflecting the struggles among the characters that ensue in the film.

Dove and Kitty (Jane Fonda) encounter one another while traveling to New Orleans from Texas. They typify drifters moving from one place to another during the Depression. They know when to hop a freight train and where to jump off to avoid railroad security guards, and are familiar with certain tricks used in those days to hitchhike along the highways. Riding the rails by hoboes was common in the Depression. They share stories about their reasons for wandering and eventually part when Dove takes a job at a roadside café owned by Teresina (Anne Baxter). Now with a salary and a room, he puts an ad in the newspaper to find Hallie. When he locates her in a brothel on Chartres Street, he attempts to rekindle a romance they had back in Texas several years ago. Jo (Barbara Stanwyck), a lesbian, owns and runs the high class brothel where Hallie now resides. Hallie is given special treatment because Jo is attracted to her.

Dove manages to convince Hallie to leave the Doll House and rents an apartment where they can live. It is on the second floor of the house at 624 Pirate's Alley (see the French Quarter Tour). Jo is well-connected with politicians and the police and refuses Hallie's plea to reunite with Dove.

The number of top stars in the film no doubt was a draw for fans but there is a glaring problem with miscasting, e.g. Anne Baxter, a natural blonde who was known for her role as the ambitious stage actress, Margo Channing, in the movie *All About Eve* (1950), plays the part of a Hispanic woman (Teresina) with a fake accent and dyed black hair. Nelson Algren's book, despite several script re-writes, fell victim to Hollywood's zeal to turn it into a movie with mass appeal. The book's setting is New Orleans during the Depression. However, the resemblance between the film and novel is minimal.

Why do both films, *The Cincinnati Kid* and *Walk on the Wild Side,* use New Orleans as a backdrop? As mentioned previously, in real life many transient people found refuge in this place. The leading players in the movie were victims of the Depression, e.g. Dove (Laurence Harvey) and Kitty (Jane Fonda) ride on railroad boxcars and hitchhike to New Orleans. And Eric (Steve McQueen) is a drifter in *The Cincinnati Kid.* Whatever shortcomings the films may have, the locations chosen in the Vieux Carré are in close proximity to Jackson Square and are historically significant. The houses in the 900 block of Chartres have been painstakingly restored and the façade and courtyard of one of the buildings were used in the movie. The second floor apartment overlooking St. Anthony's Garden symbolizes the days when the French Quarter was a bohemia for artists in the 1920s and 1930s as seen in Chapter 1 (where William Faulkner lived in 1925). The ferry on the Mississippi Riverand Preservation Hall shown in *The Cincinnati Kid* are still attractions in New Orleans.

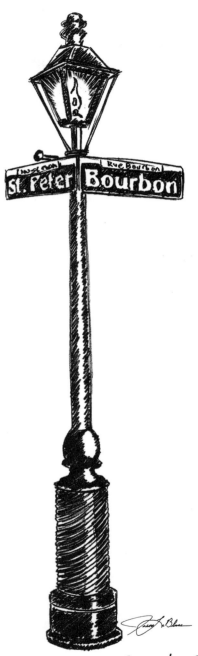

Gaslight Post in the French Quarter

CHAPTER 9

UNCLE EARL AND THE LONG MACHINE – 1928-1960

BLAZE (1989)

Earl K. Long served several terms as Governor of Louisiana. His brother Huey, whom historian Arthur M. Schlesinger, Jr. labeled "Messiah to the Redneck," crafted a style of politics which survived after his assassination in 1935. Earl never became a part of his brother's inner circle for several reasons, but was eventually to run as lieutenant-governor with Richard W. Leche in 1936 and succeeded him when the Louisiana Scandals forced Leche to resign.

Huey (popularly known as the "Kingfish") as a larger than life figure was immortalized on the screen in *All The King's Men* (1949) an adaptation of Robert Penn Warren's Pulitzer-Prize novel of the same name. It remains one of the most acclaimed motion pictures. Broderick Crawford and Mercedes McCambridge both won Oscars for acting. The film won the Oscar for Best Picture. The fictionalized character, Willy Stark, is so much like Huey that filmgoers found it difficult to separate the two men. Longism in Louisiana as a populist political movement remained a machine and is embedded in the state's history and collective memory. *All the King's Men* (2006) is a remake of the 1949 classic. Many scenes in the 2006 film were shot in New Orleans. Both films capture unique characteristics of Louisiana politics in the Huey Long era. The 2006 remake with Sean Penn as Willy Stark fell flat at the box-office, partly due to the fact that today's younger moviegoers are seven decades removed from Huey Long's pinnacle of power and have not even heard of the book *All the King's Men.*

Huey's mantle was passed down to his brother, Earl, who perpetuated the figure of a rustic champion for the common people. In *Blaze,* Paul Newman in the role of Earl K. Long during the last years in office, gives people a look at how the governor skillfully maneuvered his way through the political arena by utilizing a style reminiscent of his brother. The politics of despair upon which Huey built his empire was replaced in the 1960s with new challenges such as desegregation. Earl confronted issues with the same flamboyance as his brother.

He takes on a more human dimension when he meets Blaze Starr, a stripper at a nightclub on Bourbon Street. She finds it puzzling that the governor of the state would take an interest in her but soon develops a genuine affection for the man despite the fact that the news media condemned their relationship. The relationship became highly newsworthy. It was depicted as a disgraceful affair that played well to the public and to Earl's political opponents.

Why "Uncle Earl" chose Blaze to be a personal companion when he met her in New Orleans at the Sho-Bar Club on Bourbon Street became the subject of great interest throughout the nation. To the credit of the filmmakers, some episodes rise above the tawdry theme to present real problems in Louisiana. It is so easy to dismiss the film as an attempt to cash in on what appears to be on the surface disgraceful behavior by the governor. Upon closer examination and equipped with factual accounts in the story, a viewer can reflect upon why the Long machine was able to be so powerful for an extended period. Earl's constituents remained loyal to him even during the turbulent period in his career. For the voters, Long was a man of action who would fight for them against conservatism and elitism.

The present generation, who heard stories about Huey and Earl from their parents and grandparents, realize the serious effect Longism had on the state. The same persons know that Bourbon Street was not always a street in the Vieux Carré lined with bawdy clubs and tee shirt shops. If we take the time to walk along Bourbon before the nightly melee and look above the first floors of the buildings, it is a lesson in history (see the French Quarter Tour). At the corner of

Bourbon and Toulouse an indentation in the sidewalk (*banquette*) in front of the Ramada Hotel was a carriage space for the French Opera House. On the front wall of the hotel, a historical marker tells the story about the magnificent building that once stood on this spot (see the sketch of the Opera House). If we face the buildings across the street, notice that in terms of architectural aesthetics the upper floors still reveal that in an earlier time these buildings were luxurious residences.

Past events reveal themselves in the most improbable sites. Bourbon Street acquired the reputation as the den of the devil during World War II. Storyville was shut down in 1917. Servicemen on leave now sought out dives where they could let off steam. Today, fun-loving and partying tourists have turned the upriver blocks of Bourbon into a gathering place for revelry. Many segments in *Blaze* were filmed around Bourbon Street and other parts of the French Quarter.

In *Blaze,* the Governor seeks to recapture his youth by frequenting the clubs. When Blaze Starr enters his life, she shows sincere affection for a man in declining power and ill health. His mental illness was linked to a series of mini strokes. It is often stated in the cinema world that audiences identify with the actors on the screen in one form or another. Empathy for a figure who is suffering allows viewers to escape their own problems. As anticipated by the Hollywood movie-makers Earl's bizarre antics in the film are humorous to audiences.

When you think about the phenomenal success of the Long machine or see *All The King's Men,* consider *Blaze* as one of the last chapters in the shadow Huey Long cast on Louisiana politics. The chance encounter between the governor and a stripper on Bourbon Street allowed the local and national news media to cover it as a scandal that had widespread appeal.

As stated earlier, Earl K. Long was not included in Huey's inner circle during his brother's rule of Louisiana. However, in the film *Blaze,* Uncle Earl's conduct mirrored Huey's outlandish behavior. While in New Orleans, like his brother, Earl kept a suite of rooms at the Roosevelt Hotel to entertain his advisers and friends. Huey received important figures while dressed in silk pajamas at the Roosevelt. He caused a diplomatic blunder when he met with an admiral from Germany in this informal attire. Later, when he was informed about the uproar caused by the incident, he dressed in formal clothes to go to the admiral's ship as a gesture of apology. Both brothers were followed by an entourage of reporters and cameramen who were always looking for a story.

When Earl was photographed sitting in a grocery cart, being pushed by Blaze, it got worldwide coverage. Earl's notoriety convinced his wife Blanche and nephew

Senator Russell Long, Huey's son, to sign papers to have him committed to a state mental hospital. In the film, Blaze and his close associates remind him that he is still governor of the state. He then proceeds to fire the head of the hospital and the Secretary of Health in Baton Rouge. Then he calls the state police to help him escape. Upon his return to the capitol, many politicos worry about reprisals.

Paul Newman, even with his star status, was an odd choice to be cast as Earl. Newman exhibits Earl's erratic behavior but moviegoers are used to seeing the actor portraying younger men in other pictures.

Huey Long ruled Louisiana like a dictator and uplifted the spirits of his followers. Many astute observers believe that Franklin Delano Roosevelt's administration through the Works Progress Administration and other New Deal departments directed large appropriations to New Orleans in what is called "the Second Louisiana Purchase." Luckily for the French Quarter, a lot of this money was used to refurbish historic structures like the French Market. Before Huey was assassinated, he was acting the role of a serious challenger to F.D.R. for the Democratic Party nomination. Also, later during Earl Long's terms as governor, the Louisiana Congressional delegation chaired key committees, including Russell Long and Hale Boggs. Thus, a disproportionately large amount in federal funds were appropriated to Louisiana, in the

1950s and 1960s.

The powerful connections with congressional leaders allowed Earl K. Long to obtain appropriations from the Hill to support health care and public housing. In the film he helped black medical professionals obtain jobs in state hospitals, education, and public housing. His contemporaries accused him of catering to the black community to gain votes, but, in the movie one can see that his motivations were sincere. Desegregation of schools, buses, lunch counters, and public and privately-owned businesses presented him with a formidable task. In all of Louisiana, the most degrading elements of Jim Crow existed, including literacy tests for voting designed to exclude blacks, separate rest rooms, and even water fountains reserved for "colored" people.

Many of the visible events in the Civil Rights movement took place in New Orleans. For example, there were sit-ins at food counters in the department stores along Canal Street. Earl championed the rights of the powerless, poor black and poor white citizens in the state. The last part of *Blaze* recounts his election to the United States Congress. He dies in a shabby hotel room without knowing about his victory. He served more terms as governor of Louisiana than any other politician.

The movie *Blaze* highlights Earl Long's positive

judgments as a leader during his terms as governor. Blaze Starr is his mistress and confidante to whom he turns for encouragement during a turbulent time in Louisiana politics.

Paul Newman changes his screen idol status to play the aging Earl Long and is hailed by movie critics for his performance. The picture challenges the viewers to look beyond the tabloid coverage of the affair between Earl and Blaze. The screenplay draws heavily upon the comical aspects of the scandalous affair with Earl's question to Blaze: "Would you still love me if I wasn't the fine governor of the great State of Louisiana?" In the end, however, filmgoers witness how Earl was able to initiate progressive policies in the late 1950s and early 1960s.

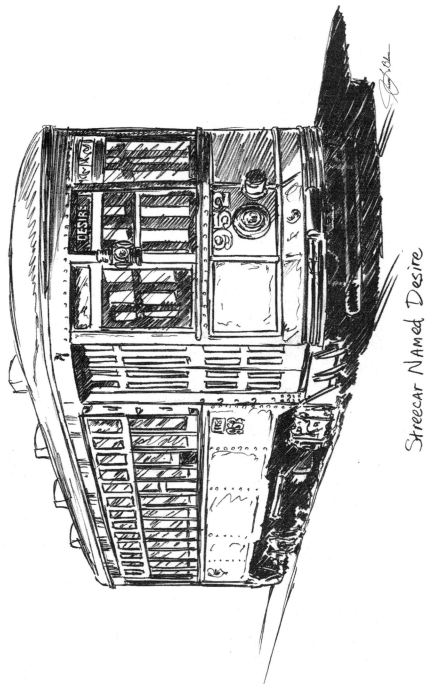

Streecar Named Desire

CHAPTER 10

A STREETCAR NAMED DESIRE – THE 1950S IN FILMS

PANIC IN THE STREETS (1950) AND A STREETCAR NAMED DESIRE (1951)

When we read Elia Kazan's autobiography and books containing interviews with the two-time Oscar winning director, what strikes us is his love affair with New Orleans. The international flavor of America's second largest seaport with its unique range of sounds, smells, and picturesque riverfront captivated Kazan. While in the city directing **Panic in the Streets**, he meandered through the streets at night listening to the sounds of jazz. When he befriended the famous musician Sidney Bechet and other jazz greats, he realized the important role of music in filmmaking. He discovered why John Ford, another famous Hollywood director, surrounded himself with rough characters. The dock workers and seamen frequenting dives along Decatur Street in the French Quarter fit naturally into his script. He wrote, "We used the city's people as our extras, and their homes, shops, and streets for scenery."

Brothels, wharves, and seedy cafes on the riverfront along the fringes of the French Quarter were more realistic than any footage shot on a Hollywood back lot. Lighting and camera crews, and cast members moved freely throughout the urban landscape. For Kazan this was a liberating experience from the rigid confines of the studios. "I learned, for instance, that film time is different from stage time." ". . . the camera is not only a recording device but a penetrating instrument. It looks into a face, not at a face."

Kazan found his four month stay in New Orleans while making *Panic in the Streets* exhilarating. The movie has a suspenseful storyline dealing with the outbreak of a plague that threatens the entire population of the city. In 1950, the streets in the French Quarter closest to the river, e.g. Decatur Street, were occupied by sleazy hotels, bars, and cafes catering to seamen who came to the port. Much of the action in the movie was shot in this area and in the storage wharves where ships docked. Today, most of the old wharves are gone.

In the film, Dr. Clinton Reed (Richard Widmark), a public health doctor, receives an urgent call from the Coroner's Office. An autopsy of a body fished from the river reveals a corpse is infected with pneumonic plague. Blackie (Jack Palance) is a local crook who has just lost money in a card game to Kochak (a minor character in the movie). Kochak is being pursued by Fitch (Zero Mostel) and another hoodlum ordered by Blackie to catch him. They shoot Kochak and throw his body into the river. In keeping with the picture's unrestrained nature, the body pulled from the water is one of Kazan's cameramen who offers to take the plunge into the river for more pay. Also, in the film a local extra eats a sandwich while taking an inoculation shot. (New Orleanians will recognize the sandwich as a "po'boy", a part of the city's culinary history).

Widmark, in cooperation with the Chief of Police (Paul Douglas), finds the ship on which Kochak was working when he came into port. All crew members on the ship are inoculated. Then, Dr. Reed and the police search for the killers who were also exposed to the plague. A chase through coffee warehouses on the docks ensues as the authorities chase Blackie and Fitch. Fitch is captured but Blackie attempts to escape by climbing a rope line tied to a ship. In a symbolic climax, Blackie loses his balance when he is unable to get past a rat guard on the rope and falls into the water. While watching the scene, the moviegoer is reminded that the "Black Death" in Europe in the Middle Ages was transmitted by fleas on rats.

After working with real dockworkers and seamen in New Orleans, Kazan used this experience when he directed **On the Waterfront**, the movie for which Marlon Brando won his first Oscar for Best Actor in

1954. It also won Oscars for Best Picture and Best Director. Kazan returned to New Orleans to shoot the opening sequence in the film version of **A *Streetcar Named Desire*** on October 26, 1950. He had directed a lengthy run of the Tennessee Williams masterpiece on Broadway (1947-1949, eight-hundred and fifty-five performances.) The play won the Pulitzer Prize and the New York Drama Critics Award.

Elia Kazan insisted that if he directed the film version of ***Streetcar***, it must open with location shots in New Orleans. His affection for the city continued as he envisioned escaping the confines of the stage. In his own words, "I'd get out of that little stage setting" and "those two miserable rooms." As the plans for the film version progressed, the parties involved with the production made a decision to hire Richard Day whose reputation as a set designer in Hollywood was held in high esteem. His credentials included a detailed knowledge of New Orleans and the French Quarter. He had seen and photographed its famed architecture on several visits to the Crescent City. His eye for detail was so sharp that he remembered seeing the old type streetcar running through the Vieux Carré on the Desire line in the 1930s and was able to describe and sketch it.

Day began to design a set in Hollywood using several hundred photographs and drawings. George James Hopkins, an Oscar winner for set decoration, followed Kazan's instructions on the construction of the Kowalski tenement with close attention to every piece of furniture - the walls, windows, and the crude nature of the place. Richard Day erected "Kazan Street" in Hollywood to re-create the director's perception of the streets around Stanley and Stella's Elysian Fields residence. Blanche Dubois in the play and movie tells her sister that "only Mr. Edgar Allan Poe - could do justice" to the shabby Elysian Fields apartment.

Jack Warner cited the need for box-office success. Reluctantly, Kazan yielded to this system under which the star quality actors were a high priority. Vivien Leigh played Blanche Du Bois in London. She was enormously popular in the United States since audiences worshipped her as Scarlett in *Gone With the Wind*. For that movie, she mastered a "Southern accent" and won the role over 1400 other actresses vying for the part. She won the Oscar for Best Actress in that role in the epic film. Jessica Tandy played Blanche in the Broadway production and Vivien Leigh had the role in the film.

The opening scene of *Streetcar* was filmed in New Orleans. Kazan used the footage during the opening credits and the first scene in the movie. On screen, a steam locomotive passenger train passes the warehouses on the riverfront into the old Louisville and Nashville train station at the foot of Canal Street. Blanche emerges from the steam clouds into the big city. The contrast between rural Mississippi and the loud bustling crowds in New Orleans sets the tone for Blanche's shock with the strange environment. Elia Kazan recounts this carefully orchestrated scene, "I would shoot Blanche's arrival at the old train station in New Orleans, materializing out of a cloud of smoke" from the old passenger train.

Outside the station, Blanche looks befuddled. In the movie a young sailor asks her, "Can I help you, ma'am?" She looks at a piece of paper while responding to his question and says, "They told me to take a streetcar named 'Desire' and transfer to one called 'Cemeteries,' ride six blocks and get off, at Elysian Fields." The Desire streetcar line stopped running through the Quarter and on Canal Street about one year before this location shooting, but the city provided a streetcar from previous eras to circle past the Louisville and Nashville Station on Canal Street. The sailor helps her board the resurrected streetcar while assuring her that this would take her to Elysian Fields Avenue. The Desire line, when it was in service, crossed Elysian Fields near Washington Park about two blocks from the 632 address. That address was used by Williams to match 632 St. Peter Street where he lived while writing *Streetcar* and where he could hear the rumbling of a local streetcar from the window of his third story studio apartment.

The Louisville and Nashville train station was still

at the foot of Canal Street when location filming took place in late October of 1950. Kazan's zeal for shooting on location surfaced once again. The cast, camera, and other crew members of the production team worked at night into the early morning hours for three days. The L&N station was still active during the daytime hours. When the Union Station on Loyola Avenue opened in 1954, the Southern Railroad and L&N stations on Canal Street closed and moved to that new facility. Both the Southern Railroad and L&N passenger terminal buildings on Canal Street were torn down. It is worth noting that today the iconic passenger train, "The City of New Orleans" running to Chicago and popularized in Arlo Guthrie's song, leaves from the Union Station.

Although Kazan was hesitant to work with Vivien Leigh, he began to like her when she accepted him as a director. Sir Laurence Olivier, her husband, had directed her performance in **Streetcar** on the stage in London. Marlon Brando's acting in the role of Stanley in the play on the New York stage overpowered Kazan. Method acting may have been new to Hollywood, but on Broadway it was widely respected. Brando was Kazan's first choice for playing the part in the film.

The New Orleans locale gave Kazan artistic freedom in a place he grew to love. He admired Tennessee Williams as a literary genius. The director saw Blanche's arrival as crucial to the success of the film. He exclaimed, "I'd make the old city's presence a force" and "create a veritable redneck Kowalski world. What a contrast to Blanche that would be! And a great lesson in filmmaking."

Williams shared the enthusiasm shown by Kazan. The movie won three Oscars for acting. Vivien Leigh won the Best Actress Oscar and Karl Malden and Kim Hunter the Oscars for Best Supporting Actors. The competition in 1951 was great. Humphrey Bogart won the Oscar for Best Actor in his role in *The African Queen*. *Streetcar* almost made a full sweep in acting. As mentioned before, Marlon Brando would have to wait until another Kazan triumph to win an Oscar for Best Actor in *On the Waterfront* in 1954. His career as film star covered five decades and made him a film legend. From *Streetcar*, he went on to diverse roles such as *The Godfather* in 1972. After his death, film historians and critics hailed him as one of the greatest actors of all time. *A Streetcar Named Desire* is now recognized as one of the top one hundred movies in cinema history by the American Film Institute.

Elia Kazan also excelled as a director. His decision to take the play to the screen remains a turning point for him. His philosophy for expanding plays from the stage to the cinema rests on his experience with *Streetcar*. Can one improve a play with cameras? His answer was "yes." He is unique among moviemakers because he leaves us written accounts about his career.

Again, his autobiography which is quoted numerous times earlier in this chapter is a valuable resource for film historians. What he writes about New Orleans and the French Quarter in the book has special meaning to anyone who loves the city. Native New Orleanians and visitors owe a debt of gratitude for his written and celluloid depictions of the city's rich and enduring history.

In his autobiography, he gives moviegoers another dimension to contemplate. When viewing the film *Streetcar,* his firsthand insights allow the audience to examine key scenes. For example, he writes, "I particularly remember the one of the naked light bulb from which Stanley had stripped the ornamental shade. Mitch turns on the light bulb and we thrust Blanche's face under its harsh light. She looks pathologically drawn and aged. This is more telling on film than on the stage." Closeup camera shots could show facial expressions never seen on the stage.

On the French Quarter tour in this book, the last stop is the spot where Blanche emerges out of the steam clouds into another world. The train station is no longer there but many natives and visitors are able to picture how it appeared.

Probably one of the most famous lines in *Streetcar* is at the end of the film. Blanche DuBois, while in an emotional state of despair and confusion, says to a doctor and nurse escorting her from the Kowalski's apartment to a car leaving for a hospital: "Whoever you are, I have always depended on the kindness of strangers."

Elia Kazan points to this famous line by Blanche as evidence of Tennessee Williams' genius as a writer and dramatist. When viewing **Panic in the Streets** and **A Streetcar Named Desire**, we can reflect upon Kazan's love for the city as a movie-maker. All of **Panic in the Streets** was filmed in New Orleans. As shown earlier Kazan insisted that the first part of **A Streetcar Named Desire** be shot in the city to give an authentic atmosphere by freeing it from the restrictions of the Broadway stage and placing it in the story's location.

119

547 Esplanade Avenue

CHAPTER 11

HOLLYWOOD IS TRANSFORMED – 1969-1970S

EASY RIDER (1969) AND CAT PEOPLE (1982)

When *Easy Rider* appeared in the theaters in 1969, no one could have predicted that it would become a cult classic. Much to the shock of the Hollywood establishment, the film with its shoestring budget of about $375,000 changed the direction of movies for the next three decades. *Easy Rider* earned over $50 million at the box-office. It was a watershed event for cinema history. It had enormous appeal to the leaders of the counterculture movement in the United States who condemned the Vietnam War, and redefined values for young people who opposed the War. During this time the older generation in the nation was appalled by the appearance of hippies, communes, draft-dodgers, peace riots on university campuses, and Woodstock. In response to voters President Richard Nixon successfully courted "the silent majority" as a force to restrain a generation attracted to drugs and "free love."

The French Quarter in New Orleans witnessed

a heavy influx of hippies after the movie appeared in theaters. Some of the key scenes in *Easy Rider* were shot on the streets in the Quarter and in St. Louis Cemetery #1 on Basin Street. The movie's soundtrack contained the counterculture anthem ***Born To Be Wild*** performed by Steppenwolf. The Roman Catholic Archdiocese of New Orleans was aghast upon learning what was filmed in its oldest cemetery. Dennis Hopper and crew did not bother to obtain a permit from the authorities to shoot the acid trip footage in the cemetery. According to those involved in making the film, Hopper took it upon himself to film the scenes in the cemetery.

For locals and visitors who have seen *Easy Rider*, the picture they remember most seems to be Peter Fonda sitting on the lap of a marble statue of a woman in the alcove of the Italian Benevolent Society Tomb. Usually, guides from the organization "Save Our Cemeteries," an organization dedicated to the preservation of historic cemeteries in New Orleans, will point out the statue as a focal point in the movie. Most people on the tour are more interested in the above ground tomb of the Voodoo Priestess, Marie Laveau, but the Italian Benevolent Society Tomb is admired for its aesthetic classical style. It is truly the largest and most beautiful monument in St. Louis Cemetery #1. Many visitors who saw *Easy Rider* and know the social impact it had on the nation want to see where the famous cemetery scenes were filmed (see a sketch of the tomb that appeared in the film).

Some accounts about Peter Fonda's weeping as he hugs the female statue say that Dennis Hopper convinced him to vent his emotions about his mother who had committed suicide when he was a youngster. The shadowy figures reciting prayers, quick shots of crosses and other religious objects during the sequence are shown along with a nude woman walking between the tombs. Hopper persuaded Toni Basil, one of the actresses, to slide along the graves in the nude. The film seems overexposed by the sun and in the background a steam machine was driving pilings into the ground for the Interstate 10 Expressway on Claiborne Avenue but the combination of flashing scenes and sound effects makes this sequence the most memorable in the movie.

Out of this chaotic camera work in the cemetery, it is almost unbelievable that any film survived. Hopper was cursing the actors and crew. The tension between Fonda and Hopper continued even after the picture was finished. Terry Southern wrote the script for the movie but Dennis Hopper denied Southern credit for his work by stating that he had been fired.

It is extremely odd that the cemetery scene in the film is often hailed as a success, but it lives up to the new wave cinematic rage in the 1960s associated with directors like the Italian genius Federico Fellini. The music, the quick movement of the camera, and the jumping from frame to frame duplicates the feeling of an acid trip. For five days about sixteen hours of footage was shot on the streets and in the cemetery in New Orleans. The result was a set of surreal images in the cemetery just outside the Quarter. Fans of the cult movie like to visit the cemetery as a location for the best-known scene in the movie.

The young actor Jack Nicholson displays a remarkable range of wisdom in his role as George Hanson. The veteran Hollywood figure Rip Torn was originally groomed for the lawyer part whom Billy (Dennis Hopper) and Captain America (Peter Fonda) meet in jail in a small Texas town. George is a lawyer who binge drinks on weekends and is well- connected with the sheriff through his family. It seems that he is routinely put behind bars after Saturday night raucous escapades, allowing him to sleep off his drunken behavior.

The two hippies in jail with him are lucky to befriend him. George is a member of the American Civil Liberties Union who defies conventional values entrenched in rural Texas and is familiar with what is taboo in small town America. He educates the bikers about the realities confronting long-haired drug users. When he arranges for their release, they invite him to ride with them to New Orleans for the Mardi Gras.

By wearing his old high school football helmet he becomes a symbol for his traditional past.

Billy complains to George, "Hey, man. All we represent to them, man, is somebody who needs a haircut." George responds: "Oh, no. What you represent to them is freedom." He knows his weekend drunken partying is tolerated, but is aware that hippie lifestyle, when flaunted in redneck society, is perceived as an evil by the rustics living in towns from Texas to Louisiana. The counterculture figures threaten to destroy the rural male conventional world.

When the bikers try to get a meal in a café in Morganza, Louisiana, upriver from New Orleans, four teenage girls infatuated with their appearance call them "cute." Some roughnecks in another booth begin to taunt them. George's earlier prophecy is fulfilled when the townspeople see the hippies' "freedom" as a danger to society.

As the four teenage girls giggle and follow them outside the café to ask about their motorcycles, the element of danger heightens because the misfits seem to be corrupting the youth by exposing them to a new lifestyle. It should be mentioned here that the use of amateurs as figures in the movie becomes quite obvious in these scenes. One cost-cutting method for the film was having locals appear in the footage. That night as the three camp out along the side of a highway in sleeping bags, they are attacked and beaten by hicks as they sleep. After a shocking tragedy occurs the two 'easy riders" go to New Orleans.

George had already shown them a card he said the governor of Louisiana gave him. It advertises "Madame Tinkertoy's House of Blue Lights" on the corner of Bourbon and Toulouse in the French Quarter. According to George, "Now, this is supposed to be the finest whorehouse in the South." As we see in Chapter 7, Storyville gave New Orleans a reputation as a city which tolerates vices. When they go to the brothel they meet two attractive prostitutes played by Karen Black and Toni Basil.

Some film historians praise *Easy Rider* for creating a new Hollywood with a new breed of directors such as Peter Bogdanvich, Francis Ford Coppola, George Lucas, Martin Scorsese, Steven Speilberg, and Paul Schrader. Others argue the film was so filled with infighting during its production between Hopper and Fonda and so fragmented that it was incredible that it was finally finished. Although new doors were opened for experimentation, its impact on the film industry was not welcomed by the Hollywood establishment.

At the Cannes Film Festival *Easy Rider* won an award for Best New Film. At the Oscar ceremonies, *The French Connection* won Best Picture, and Gene Hackman received the Best Actor award. The studios did take notice of Jack Nicholson's nomination for Best Supporting Actor. Paramount Pictures and others in Hollywood viewed the movie as an indicator that the old system had to adapt to dealing with the unique issues raised by *Easy Rider*. The American Film Institute places it in the top one hundred films of the century. It did indeed change Tinseltown in a dramatic fashion by allowing filmmakers to cover subjects previously considered to be taboo.

Easy Rider (1969), *Walk on the Wild Side* (1962), and *Jezebel* (1938), all films connected to New Orleans, complete the trilogy for the Fonda acting dynasty when Peter, Jane and Henry appear respectively in these three movies. Their performances in the pictures are now part of cinematic history. From biker to banker with a brothel in between, their movie roles could not be more different.

Paul Schrader was one of the bold new directors in the 1970s and 1980s. According to Peter Biskins, his meteoric rise to prominence was accompanied by destructive behavior associated with cocaine use. His *American Gigolo* in 1980 was a huge success at the box-office. In 1982, New Orleans became the location for his horror movie *Cat People*. Schrader was able to assemble an outstanding cast including Natassia Kinski, Malcolm McDowell and John Heard. In the original version in 1942, Jacques Tourneur's *Cat People* was highly acclaimed as a film noir classic. Simone

Simon was hailed for her role as a figure haunted by her fate as a member of a tribe who offered up women to leopards to please the gods. The leopards mated with the women to produce "cat people" in human form. These same "cat people" were destined to mate with their own kind when transformed into leopards while under a spell. Sounds, shadows and lights keep the viewers in suspense, but leopards are never shown on the screen in the 1942 *Cat People*.

Paul Schrader used the Vieux Carré's macabre atmosphere in a color version with the same story and filmed some parts of the picture at the Old Audubon Zoo (see the St. Charles Avenue streetcar tour). Irena (Natassia Kinski) is stalked by her brother Paul (Malcolm McDowell) who is transformed into a black leopard as he preys upon women whom he tears apart. Irena soon realizes that she is a "cat person" condemned to mating with one of her own kind. In this case her brother is the last of the "cat people" and her only choice as a mate. She falls in love with Oliver (John Heard), a veterinarian at the Audubon Park Zoo.

Nudity, blood, raging black leopards, and haunting music along with dream sequences result in a bizarre set of events. The movie is both ghastly and fascinating. A historic mansion on Esplanade Avenue (547, see the French Quarter tour and sketch) serves as the home for the brother and sister. Female (pronounced "fah mahl lee") played by Ruby Dee is the housekeeper. She adds an element of voodoo by practicing occult rituals and protecting gruesome remains of victims in the basement. She wears traditional African-Caribbean clothing and a headscarf like those historically adorning voodoo priestesses. She also serves gumbo, a dish identified with New Orleans' multi-diversity.

The theme music, "Putting Out the Fire," written and sung by David Bowie sets the mood for scenes that virtually assault the audience. When Joe, one of the zookeepers (Ed Begley, Jr.), has his arm ripped from his body while feeding a caged black leopard, viewers are conditioned for future bloody and gory pictures. Hitchcock's *Psycho* in 1960 seemed to have raised the bar for frightening scenes in films. *Cat People* is a good example of how far filmmakers will go to shock viewers. The eerie night footage shot in the French Quarter and swamps around Lake Catherine near the city bring the production to a new height for the horror genre.

Easy Rider and *Cat People* both appealed to the younger generation of the 1970s and 1980s. Nudity, drug use, and violence are unbridled in the pictures. Peter Buskind calls the new filmmakers "movie brats." His book *Easy Riders, Raging Bulls* gives us many stories about new directors who came forward when the studios in Hollywood were going bankrupt.

1018 Royal St.

CHAPTER 12

A CITY OF MUSIC – A TIMELESS TRADITION

THE BIG EASY (1987) AND KING CREOLE (1959)

It is often said that music is the glue that holds multicultural New Orleans together. In the Vieux Carré, jazz nightclubs such as Preservation Hall feature traditional jazz as it was played in its early days. In some cases, youngsters receive formal training at the New Orleans Center For the Creative Arts. Wynton Marsalis and Harry Connick, Jr. are both products of NOCCA. These musicians learned their skills from jazz players from the older generation. Ellis Marsalis, father of jazz-playing sons, taught at NOCCA. Many who left New Orleans, as did Louis Armstrong, still express loyalty to their jazz roots.

Sidney Bechet found fame in Paris but always remembered the city where he perfected his talent. Louis Armstrong came back to reign as the King of the Zulu Parade in 1949, long after he achieved international fame.

Day and night street musicians entertain visitors to the French Quarter with a wide variety of native musical forms. The French Quarter Festival held a few weeks before the Jazz and Heritage Festival, is another popular event for music fans, and now, in August, the Satchmo Summer Fest adds another major event to the festivals of music in the city.

Two films shot in the New Orleans area focusing on music are *King Creole* and *The Big Easy*. *King Creole* is based on Harold Robbins' book *A Stone for Danny Fischer*. The story about a troubled teenager is set in Chicago, but the filmmakers decided that New Orleans would be more appealing to moviegoers because of the city's unique architecture and musical heritage. Among the many movies featuring Elvis Presley, this is perhaps the best. The songs "King Creole", "Trouble," and "As Long As I Have You" are rock and roll tunes performed by Elvis. The title song "King Creole" and the King Creole Club on Bourbon Street where Elvis sings give the film its name. Elvis starred in 31 motion pictures. *King Creole* is recognized by his fans as one of his top 4 films.

A strong supporting cast in *King Creole*, including Walter Matthau and Carolyn Jones, help carry the story of a high school dropout who rises from a job cleaning up clubs to a singing star on Bourbon Street. Blackmail, gang activity, and romantic interludes surround the singer as he seeks to make it in show business. Today, many film historians praise the movie as a "new classic."

In the beginning of the movie, when Elvis harmonizes from a gallery on Royal Street (see walking tour), with a woman in a mule drawn wagon selling crawfish, an old tradition in the French Quarter is revealed. It was customary for street vendors to sell berries, charcoal, and even clothespoles to residents. These figures are captured in paintings, photographs, and prints as part of life in earlier days in the Quarter.

Rock and roll music was at the time very popular in New Orleans. Fats Domino is the best known New Orleans entertainer in this musical field. Irma Thomas and the late Professor Longhair are two others who are revered by locals for sharing their talent with generations in the city. Radio stations and recording studios in New Orleans specializing in rock and roll are abundant. Several homegrown artists are in the Rock and Roll Hall of Fame. Elvis Presley viewed Fats Domino as "the Father of Rock and Roll."

The Big Easy (1987) is an action-packed, romantic film about police corruption in the French Quarter, showcasing New Orleans and Cajun music. Remy McSwain (Dennis Quaid) is a flirtatious detective with a horrendous Cajun accent. The accent makes native New Orleanians cringe because it sends a message that the populace speaks in this fashion. Even people in Cajun parts of Louisiana do not speak like Remy. Anne Osborn (Ellen Barkin) is an assistant district attorney investigating mob murders and police corruption.

Remy takes Anne to Tipitina's (a famous music club) while enticing her into what becomes a steamy love affair.

Aaron Neville's song, "Tell It Like It Is" and other musical pieces make the soundtrack from the movie very popular. Among the films covered in this book, this one stands out as one filled with popular tunes. "Zydeco Gris Gris" by Beausoleil, "Tipitina" by Professor Longhair, "Iko Iko" sung by the Dixie Cups, and other compositions have made the soundtrack album extremely popular. The album on a compact disc is still available.

According to the local newspaper, the Times-Picayune, the term "The Big Easy" may be traced to a dance hall or a dance of the same name which existed earlier in the city's history. Today, the nickname "The Big Easy" has been adopted as an endearing label for New Orleans along with "The Crescent City" and "The City That Care Forgot."

In one part of the movie, the St. Augustine High School Marching Band is shown practicing on the neutral ground, or grassy median, in front of Remy's apartment. The "Marching One Hundred" is playing "Little Liza Jane." This band has appeared at numerous high profile football games and in many parades, especially during Mardi Gras.

Remy sums up the image often cultivated by the

tourism industry when he says to Anne Osborn, "Just relax, darling.' This is the Big Easy. Folks have a certain way o' doin' things down here."

Both **King Creole** and **The Big Easy** exemplify a local passion for music. The legendary Louis Armstrong personifies this affection for New Orleans and its music. Armstrong's love for red beans and rice, a traditional native dish, usually served on Mondays (by custom the day when the wash is done while the beans cook) always closed his letters with the melodious ending "Red Beans and Ricely Yours."

Louisiana Supreme Court Building

CHAPTER 13

CONSPIRACY MOVIES IN NEW ORLEANS

DOUBLE JEOPARDY (1999) AND JFK (1991)

Tommy Lee Jones, the Oscar-winning actor, appears in two movies with sequences shot in New Orleans. Both films have suspenseful plots and subplots. In *JFK* he is Clay Shaw, the central figure in Jim Garrison's investigation of President Kennedy's assassination. In *Double Jeopardy* (1999), he stars along with Ashley Judd. Several parts of the mystery movie were shot in the French Quarter and in the Garden District. Libby (Judd) is framed for the murder of her husband in Washington State. While serving time in prison, she discovers that not only is her husband alive, but also he engineered his disappearance from a sailboat on which they were aboard. Blood and weapons on the boat discovered by the police lead them to charge her with murder. A fellow inmate in prison tells her about double jeopardy, the constitutional guarantee forbidding the courts from trying a person for the same crime twice.

When she is released from prison, Travis (Tommy Lee Jones) becomes her parole officer. She traces her son and husband to New Orleans. After escaping from Travis' custody, she travels to the city where she finds that her husband, under an assumed name, owns a hotel in the French Quarter (the historic Hermann-Grima House on St. Louis Street is used as the site for the hotel in the film). She confronts her husband in his office in the hotel with a gun demanding that he tell her the whereabouts of their son. He persuades her to meet him at a cemetery where he will return the boy to her. In Lafayette Cemetery #1, following a jazz funeral, she wanders around to the middle until she sees a youngster posing as the son sitting by a grave. The husband knocks her unconscious.

What takes place next in this suspense picture could only happen in New Orleans. Upon waking up from unconsciousness, she finds herself in a coffin inside an above-ground tomb. She manages to free herself from the tomb. Travis (Tommy Lee Jones) also discovers that her husband is living in New Orleans under a false name. Judd and Jones approach him with the charges against him. After he is shot while resisting, he is taken into custody. Libby (Judd) is reunited with her son at a military academy. The unique local custom of above-ground burial adds to the riveting plot as it unfolds. As a footnote to this it is worth pointing out that on July 14, 1995, Anne Rice staged a fake funeral at Lafayette Cemetery #1 (the same cemetery used in **Double Jeopardy)** to publicize her book, **Memnoch**

the Devil. Rice was in a coffin as the procession made its way to the book signing party at the Garden District Book Shop across the street.

Oliver Stone's box-office hit, ***JFK*** (1991) is based on real life characters including Clay Shaw, played by Tommy Lee Jones. Shaw was a prominent business leader and preservationist who lived in the French Quarter. He became a target for New Orleans District Attorney Jim Garrison's attempt to prove that he and others were involved in a conspiracy to assassinate President Kennedy in Dallas in 1963. In terms of history the movie challenges the Warren Commission's argument that Lee Harvey Oswald was a lone gunman. Film critics hold it up as an example of the power that Hollywood has over public opinion. A majority of Americans still do not accept the Warren Commission Report. It may be said in this case, everyone loves a conspiracy!

Stone's clever use of the Zapruder footage of the event and underscoring the mistakes or omissions in the Report turns ***JFK*** into a strong propaganda piece. The History Channel aired the controversy in a series called "From Real to Reel." This program has been shown repeatedly on Sundays in recent years. The commentators on the program point out that most historians agree with the Warren Commission, but admit that a large number of moviegoers who saw ***JFK*** had their beliefs about a conspiracy solidified.

For a thorough and enlightening account about this controversial movie one can read ***JFK: The Book of the Film*** (1992). It contains the documented screenplay and numerous articles by historians, film critics, filmmakers, journalists, and politicians who defend or attack the movie.

New Orleans and the French Quarter are center stage in *JFK*. Kevin Costner, playing Jim Garrison, goes to the Napoleon House on the corner of Chartres and St. Louis Streets to see the television coverage of the assassination in Dallas. His office in the Louisiana State Supreme Court Building on Royal is near this famous bar and restaurant. There are two scenes shot at Antoine's Restaurant and several others on French Quarter streets and in the Garden District.

Much of the movie is based on Jim Garrison's book ***On the Trail of the Assassins*** and a lengthy two year trial of Clay Shaw. The national media covered the proceedings on a daily basis. Stone was able to use an actual case and a group of New Orleans figures who were accused of being part of a conspiracy. These factors contributed to the dramatic impact the film had on the audience. The conspiratorial story tries to connect Jack Ruby with Clay Shaw and other local figures to what President Eisenhower called "the military-industrial complex." The theory in a convoluted way puts Kennedy's decision to end the Vietnam War as the primary reason for his assassination.

Lee Harvey Oswald, who was born and raised in New Orleans, is depicted as a fall guy for the national plot. In the movie Oswald (Gary Oldman), is shown handing out leaflets for an organization called "Fair Play For Cuba" on Canal Street shortly before the assassination. The movie also contains interviews Oswald gave to radio and television stations in New Orleans during that time.

The cast is filled with big name stars, Tommy Lee Jones, nominated for a Best Actor Oscar for playing Clay Shaw, Kevin Costner (Garrison), Sissy Spacek (Mrs. Garrison), Gary Oldman (Lee Harvey Oswald), Jack Lemmon (Jack Martin), Ed Asner (Guy Bannister), and Walter Matthau (Senator Russell Long), and many more well-known actors.

The power of films over public opinion is demonstrated by *JFK*. It won Oscars for cinematography and film-editing. The federal government declassified sealed documents one year after the picture was shown in theaters and the Congress conducted hearings on the Warren Commission's credibility as the document of record for President John F. Kennedy's assassination. Both events led to numerous probes into whether this case should be re-examined. New forensic technology not available forty years ago was used in various ways. Computer modeling and examination of the Zapruder footage frame by frame showing how a single bullet could have passed through both the President's and

Governor Connelly's bodies supported "the lone gunman theory" in the Warren Commission's report. But no television documentary or book is capable of putting public skepticism to rest. Polls indicate that a majority of people in the nation still do not accept the Commission's conclusions. If everyone loves a conspiracy, then **JFK** stirred the kettle of doubt still existing more than forty years after the fact.

The movie ignites the audience's emotions when Jim Garrison (Kevin Costner) tells the jury: "The ghost of John F. Kennedy confronts us with the secret murder at the heart of the American dream. He forces on us the appalling questions: Of what is our Constitution made? What is the future of democracy...?" People who lived through Kennedy's assassination can say where they were when they heard the news about the President's death.

In **Double Jeopardy** a husband tries to get away with a plot that sends his wife to jail for his murder. She finds him alive in New Orleans under a new name. Libby, with help from her parole officer, Travis, eventually finds her son at a boarding school. The suspenseful film is very entertaining as it unfolds in New Orleans. **JFK,** crafted by master filmmaker Oliver Stone, has no happy ending for audiences. It opens up many conspiracy theories on President Kennedy's assassination for better or worse. New Orleans becomes the center for conspirators. After several decades, we wonder about what impact *JFK* will have upon movie fans who were born after November 1963. In the press, many journalists accuse Oliver Stone of re-writing history in what they call a clever "docudrama" that uses footage of real events.

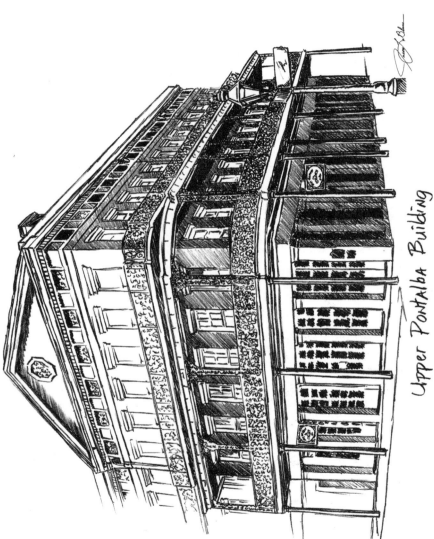

Upper Pontalba Building

CHAPTER 14

JOHN GRISHAM IN NEW ORLEANS

THE PELICAN BRIEF (1993) AND RUNAWAY JURY (2003)

John Grisham, one of today's most prolific writers, was born in Arkansas in 1955 but moved to Mississippi in 1967. He completed his undergraduate degree at Mississippi State University and went on to earn a law degree from the University of Mississippi. He served as a Representative in the Mississippi Legislature and began writing novels on legal intrigues. His book ***The Firm*** was made into a movie directed by Sydney Pollack. The film established him as storyteller who captured the imaginations of audiences by enthralling them with the intrigues found in the legal profession. Devotees of his books lamented changes made to his novels in screen adaptations but his reputation in print and in films elevated him to celebrity status.

Two of his best selling books, ***The Pelican Brief*** and ***Runaway Jury,*** used New Orleans as the setting when they were made into films. Earlier we saw that film directors like to show audiences images of New Orleans on the screen. The book, ***The Pelican Brief***, is set in the city but ***Runaway Jury*** takes place in

Biloxi, Mississippi. John Grisham uses New Orleans in several of his novels. The city lends itself to mystery and intrigue, and Hollywood knows this. *The Pelican Brief* (1993) is a suspense-filled production with many action sequences taking place in the French Quarter. This thrilling movie takes liberties with location sites. For example, the exterior shots of Antoine's restaurant are made to look as though it is across the street from a parking lot in the Warehouse District, whereas in reality it is on St. Louis Street in the French Quarter.

When Darby (Julia Roberts) tries to convince her lover that he is too intoxicated to drive after dinner at Antoine's, he refuses to let her drive him home in his car. When he turns on the ignition, the car explodes into a fireball (the explosion, as we saw before, takes place in a parking lot in the Warehouse District). Darby helplessly watches from across the street. Her lover is a Tulane law professor (Sam Shepard), clerked for one of two Supreme Court justices who are mysteriously murdered in Washington. She wrote a paper leading to a theory about the killings called *The Pelican Brief*. She shares it with her professor who forwards it to friends in Washington. Her research is so close to the truth that she and her lover become a threat to powerful figures in the federal government including the President.

After the explosion she realizes that her life is in danger. To avoid would-be assassins, she meets a classmate at a crowded bar in the Quarter and tells her to attend the professor's funeral services and to tell whomever asks about her that she is no longer in the city. As Darby moves from one hotel to another on Canal Street, her friend attends the services held in St. Anthony's Garden behind St. Louis Cathedral, and says to people that Darby has left to visit relatives.

Darby makes arrangements to meet one of her professor's friends at the Spanish Plaza at the foot of Canal Street. Much to her surprise, she is met at the crowded plaza by a paid assassin who just murdered her contact. He is shot by F.B.I. agents as he attempts to murder her. The rest of the story has her seeking help from a Washington journalist named Gray Grantham (Denzel Washington). He protects her as they uncover the facts about the conspirators who arranged the killings of the two justices.

The film is directed by Alan J. Pakula whose credits include the Oscar-winning film *Sophie's Choice* (1982.) The movie follows the book for the most part since Darby's theory is traced to a case brought to court by a young environmentalist in Louisiana. He attempts to expose oil corporations which made large political contributions to the President, who is in the position to appoint Supreme Court Justices with lenient policies concerning oil drilling in the Louisiana wetlands.

In the novel, **Runaway Jury**, the legal issue of the story is a class action suit against giant tobacco companies set in Biloxi, Mississippi. The filmmakers changed the location to New Orleans. The Louisiana Supreme Court Building in the center of the French Quarter becomes the main cinema site and the case is against corporations producing assault weapons. The filmmakers liked the location so much that nearly sixty sites in the French Quarter are used in the production. Gene Hackman and Dustin Hoffman bring star power to the movie. As with **Panic in the Streets** in 1950, the city is center stage. In a twenty-first century cinematic world, the enduring charm of the French Quarter continues to interest moviegoers.

Nick Easter (John Cusack) and his girlfriend Marlee (Rachel Weisz) work inside and outside the courtroom to influence the jury to find gun manufacturers guilty of selling assault weapons to anyone who can afford them, even without background checks on customers.

In **Runaway Jury**, Gene Hackman appears in his third role in movies based on Grisham's novels (**The Firm** and **The Chamber** are the other two). Using sophisticated equipment, Rankin Fitch (Hackman) assembles a crew in an abandoned French Quarter building to profile prospective jurors for the trial in an attempt to get a favorable jury for his clients. At one point in the picture, Fitch tells his staff: "Gentlemen, trials are too important to be left up to juries." We can contrast this cynical view on juries with the film *12 Angry Men* (1957). In that picture Henry Fonda, as a juryman, tries to talk the other 11 members of a jury to think about being too quick about finding a boy guilty of a murder. Wendell Rohr (Hoffman) in *Runaway Jury* represents a woman whose husband was killed by assault weapons in the husband's office a few years earlier.

As mentioned, the Louisiana Supreme Court Building, an imposing structure in the Beaux Arts style that takes up an entire block of the French Quarter, is the venue for the trial. The Napoleon House on St. Louis and Chartres Streets and the Pontalba Café on Jackson Square are two other historic sites used in the film.

Another top selling novel by John Grisham turned into a movie is *The Client* (1994). Part of this movie used New Orleans as a filming location. Susan Saradon (*Pretty Baby*) and Tommy Lee Jones (*Double Jeopardy* and *JFK*) star in the picture. Novelist Grisham and screenwriters seem to be attracted to the Crescent City locale.

French Opera House

CHAPTER 15

CONCLUSION: HOLLYWOOD SOUTH

In this book, we have seen how filmmakers make New Orleans a "character" in films. Also, for posterity the city is shown during several historic periods when the cameras record these ages on location or on a studio backlot. For the viewers, what they see on the screen serves as a record of how things in New Orleans may have appeared in past ages. For example: Do we learn something about how people lived in colonial times from the film ***Interview With the Vampire*** or how the 1853 yellow fever epidemic affected the city's population in the movie ***Jezebel***? What do we learn about the free people of color and *plaçage* when watching ***The Feast of All Saints*** and ***Saratoga Trunk***? We may see these pictures several times before we can answer these questions. But for the movie enthusiasts, this is part of the fun of discovering new things in films.

The actors in the twenty movies challenge us to think about the past and become as the expression goes "a fly on the wall" or a witness of history. The actors and the stories in which they appear let us use our imaginations to the fullest. In Hollywood over the years, the actors in the films covered have been recognized as being at the top of their profession. Bette Davis, Vivien Leigh, Gary Cooper, Ingrid Bergman, Marlon Brando, Jack Nicholson, Jane Fonda, Gene Hackman, and Dustin Hoffman have all been honored with two or more Oscars for acting along with numerous nominations in the same category. Bette Davis and Vivien Leigh won Oscars for their roles in *Jezebel* and *A Streetcar Named Desire*. For Marlon Brando, his role as Stanley Kowalski in *Streetcar* is a defining part for a star who became a cinema legend. Jack Nicholson and Jane Fonda established themselves as screen performers in *Easy Rider* and *Walk on the Wild Side*.

Two of the films covered are on the American Film Institute's top one hundred movies, *A Streetcar Named Desire* and *Easy Rider*. It seems likely that New Orleans will continue to earn its recent fame as "Hollywood South" as more moviemakers choose the city as a location. Tax credits from the State of Louisiana also give incentives to the film industry. The local newspaper, *The Times-Picayune*, now features a weekly column titled "Hollywood South" telling its readers about street closings where filming is taking place, who is in town from the movie industry, and news about upcoming cinema productions.

In a time when the cinematic world is dominated

by multiplexes in America's suburbs, it is appropriate for movie fans to be nostalgic about the small neighborhood theatres of yesteryear. In 1950 in New Orleans, there were still over fifty neighborhood theatres in existence. In addition, on and around Canal Street many picture palaces were showing first-run movies. While the yearning for these days is limited to older generations, one can take comfort in the fact that film is studied as an art form and is an integral part of the curriculum at colleges and universities and is studied at the high school level. This book attempts to cover only a few films shot in New Orleans or duplicated on sets at studios. A wide spectrum of movie genres is included in the hope that readers will be able to pick and choose some of their favorite pictures.

Films breathe life into previous times. An example of this is a sequence in **Saratoga Trunk** when Clio Dulaine (Ingrid Bergman), her maid (Flora Robson), and her coachman (Jerry Austin) stroll through the French Quarter in the 1870s. They hear melodies sung by street vendors, smell the aromas of the city, and taste jambalaya at the French Market. Their walk allows filmgoers to identify with the characters in the story. Under the market's arcades, a strikingly beautiful Clio who was raised in elegant Paris meets Clint Maroon (Gary Cooper), a personification of the Old West in America. She is dressed in fine clothes from France and he wears boots and a wide-brimmed hat. Her maid, Angelique, dismisses him as a "cowboy". But Clio admires the rugged good looks of this tall stranger. The French Market serves as a background to this encounter. It is filled with vegetables, fruit, live birds in cages, and seafood offered up in foreign-sounding languages from stalls and baskets. Lake shrimp, soft-shelled crabs, fish from the Gulf of Mexico and other local delicacies are on display. The scene takes us back to an age when New Orleans teemed with the excitement and bustle of a prosperous international port. (The French Market is the first stop on the French Quarter Tour.)

We saw earlier that in the 1920s and 1930s writers and artists were drawn to the eccentric lifestyle of the French Quarter. Streetcars were a part of the city's landscape before Tennessee Williams wrote *A Streetcar Named Desire*. Desire Street was the turning around point for the streetcar carrying its name as it rolled on tracks parallel to the Mississippi. In both the play and the movie, Stanley Kowalski (Marlon Brando) represents the working class living along the route. Blanche DuBois (Vivien Leigh) is puzzled by his odd Polish name and crude behavior. She calls him "common." He acts like a primitive "caveman" not like a "gentleman" of Old South mythology. Stanley reacts to her pretentious behavior by using Huey Long's slogan "every man a king" and Louisiana's Napoleonic Code to back up his arguments with her. Williams' dramatic tale uses metaphors of a time and place. New Orleans is again both a character and a stage for the narrative. (On the St. Charles Avenue tour, we ride on a historic streetcar like the one taken by Blanche in the film.)

We moviegoers often develop an emotional attachment to what we see on the screen. Most travel guidebooks about New Orleans focus on the city's history, culture, food, and architecture. Most first time visitors have only seen the city depicted on the big screen or at home watching videos. The sketches, tours, and maps in this book let us ask questions about how we form images of New Orleans.

Now we turn our attention to walking and streetcar tours to stir our imaginations about New Orleans' rich history, culture, and architecture to find out why filmmakers like to make the city both a stage and a character in movies.

French Quarter Courtyard

FRENCH QUARTER TOUR OF MOVIE SITES

Wear comfortable shoes and clothes suitable for the weather. The French Quarter is compact in size and pedestrian-friendly. The sketches in this book were designed to give us images of some of the places on the map. If we walk slowly, we will be able to see elaborate ironworks, carriageways (porte cocheres), and courtyards. The Quarter is an outdoor museum and home to several thousand residents. Writers and artists are inspired by unique treasures found around every corner. A café or coffee shop with a good view provides a refreshing break and a chance to reflect upon why filmmakers like to use this section of the city as a backdrop for movies. Because touring the whole Quarter takes 3 to 4 hours and is physically demanding, the tour is divided into 3 sections: the lower and upper Quarter and nearby the Quarter.

If movie buffs find themselves at sites on this tour where it feels like *déjà vu*, perhaps it is because they remember the site from a scene in a film

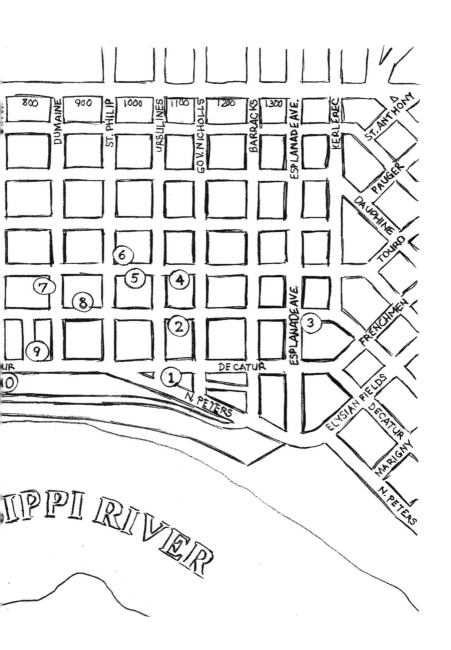

800 900 DUMAINE ST. PHILIP 1000 URSULINES 1100 GOV. NICHOLLS 1200 BARRACKS 1300 ESPLANADE AVE. KERLEREC ST. ANTHONY PAUGER DAUPHINE TOURO FRENCHMEN ESPLANADE AVE. DECATUR N. PETERS ELYSIAN FIELDS DECATUR MARIGNY N. PETERS

MISSISSIPPI RIVER

French Market in the 1870's

LOWER QUARTER

We start on the corner of North Peters and Ursulines Streets. At the Farmer's Market, one can recall scenes from **Saratoga Trunk**. This romantic film stars Ingrid Bergman and Gary Cooper. Clio Dulaine (Bergman), her maid, and man servant walk through the French Market of the 1870s. This is the oldest city market in the United States. A quick look at the map shows that the market runs along the edge of the Mississippi River for six blocks. Imagine how it must have looked and sounded in the early days with Choctaw Indians selling filé for gumbo (ground sassafras leaves), bay leaves, medicinal herbs, and baskets; African women singing about the freshness of the berries they were peddling; Sicilian men offering fruits, vegetables, and seafood; German butchers displaying various kinds of meats; French vendors shouting the praises of birds in cages for the dining table; and Spaniards in stalls crying out the names of many cooked local dishes.

The market at that time was a medley of accents and foreign tongues, and filled with a cornucopia of foods, which to the untrained ear resembled a new Tower of Babel! Today, the arches of the French Market are lined with an assortment of locally-grown vegetables, fruits, and spices harkening back to the

Ursuline Convent

past, and a modern day Flea Market is found at the end of the market.

At the corner of Ursulines Street cross Chartres, the street names provide a lesson in history in three languages – English and French on the lantern posts, and later Spanish on glazed tiles set into the sides of buildings along the way. At the corner of Ursulines and Chartres Streets, you will see the old Ursuline Convent - the oldest building in the lower Mississippi Valley. You can visualize the sisters keeping a vigil of prayer all night at the statue of Our Lady of Prompt Succor (Quick Help) during the Battle of New Orleans in 1815. There is a memorable depiction of the battlefield in *The Buccaneer*.

Six Ursuline nuns arrived in New Orleans in 1727 after a hazardous trip across the Atlantic on a sailing ship from France. This order of sisters came from Rouen to the New World to educate girls and care for the sick. The imposing convent was completed in 1745 and is a good example of French colonial architecture. Notice the steep roof (built for snow that never came), chimneys, and the small dormers. The builders followed plans found in a military handbook and the result looks as though it belongs in Canada rather than New Orleans. It survived the two great fires in 1788 and 1794. The nuns occupied the Convent from 1734 until 1814 (ninety years). The building is now open for tours. It belongs to the Catholic Archdiocese of New

547 Esplanade Avenue

Orleans.

🎥 **3** 🎥 We turn right on the corner of Ursulines and Chartres Streets. Across the street from the Convent is the Beauregard-Keyes House (1826). Adjacent to the Convent is St. Mary's Church (1846), one of the oldest church buildings in New Orleans. Along the way to Esplanade Avenue at 1132 Chartres is the Soniat House Hotel (1829), five Greek Revival houses in the 1200 block, and three kinds of shotgun houses (single, side-gallery, and double) in the 1300 block. A shotgun is a house without a hall. The doors are lined up in a row. On the corner of Chartres and Esplanade, look at the stately mansion across the neutral ground (median). Several scenes in *Cat People* were filmed here at 547 Esplanade (an Italiante home built in 1879).

🎥 **4** 🎥 As we turn left on Esplanade, in the middle of the block at 616 Esplanade is a type of house which was popular from 1870 through 1910 during the Victorian era. During this period homes were decorated with brackets. When we reach Royal Street, we turn left. Look at the large residence on the corner. It is noted for its intricate iron railings. As we walk up Royal Street, we can see a detached two-story structure behind the main house locally referred to as a *garçonnière*, slave quarters, or service wing. In the movie *Saratoga Trunk*, Clio's (Ingrid Bergman's) home on Rampart Street has this feature. At 1124

Royal stands a house with lots of gingerbread decorations in the Eastlake style. On the corner in the next block at 1140 Royal, we see the Madame La Laurie House. This home is linked to a legend about a fire in 1834. According to the story (which would be a good, ready-made film script), at the time of the fire the mistress of the home on this site fled away from the city when it was discovered that she was torturing slaves even to the point of death. In the same block, the Gallier House Museum (1132 Royal) is said to be the model for the townhouse occupied by Lestat and Louis in *Interview With the Vampire*. The courtyard here is a serene oasis away from the street noises. However, during the early history of the city, the patios and courtyards in the Quarter were workplaces for cooking and doing laundry.

We continue on Royal and slow down to look at the second floor of the gallery at 1018 Royal. This is where Danny (Elvis Presley in *King Creole*) harmonizes with a woman in a horse-drawn wagon as she shouts out that she is selling crawfish. Hawkers of fruits, rice fritters (*calas*), eggs, berries, and other goods called out to the residents in the old Creole neighborhood with rhymes and song. Some of the street vendors were still present in the Quarter in the 1950s when this film was made. In the opening scenes of *King Creole*, several of these street vendors sing about berries, tomatoes, and gumbo.

Gallier House

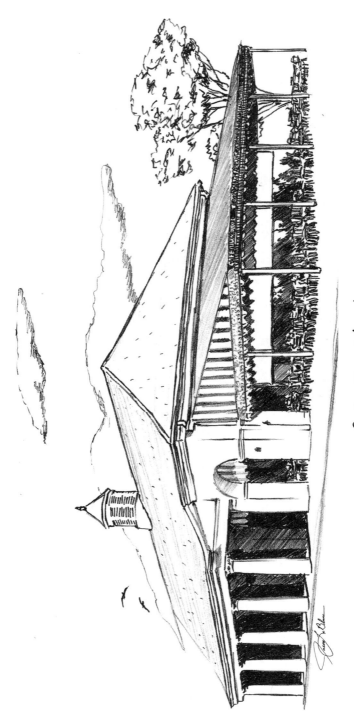

Café Du Monde

6 Also in *King Creole*, Danny (Elvis) attends Royal High School in the building on the corner of St. Philip and Royal (McDonogh 15 Public School). Many children of Sicilian immigrants went to this school in the early twentieth century. These children lived in the French Quarter near the school.

7 We turn left on to Dumaine Street and look for 632, Madame John's Legacy (1788) that served as a location for sequences in *Interview With a Vampire*. This West Indies-style house, named after a fictitious character, is now a museum operated by the State of Louisiana. Across the street there are three houses which are examples of Creole cottages. This type of house is found throughout the Quarter. At one time in the 1830s and 1840s, as much as one-third of the property in the French Quarter was owned by the free women of color and many of their houses were Creole cottages. We see Creole cottages in the film *The Feast of All Saints*.

8 We continue on Dumaine to Chartres where we turn left. Although in *Walk on the Wild Side* 904 Chartres was given as the address of the brothel called Doll House, the actual address on Chartres is 931. This townhouse was used during the filming of the movie.

9 We turn around and go back to Dumaine Street. We turn left on Dumaine and proceed to

Decatur Street. Turning right on Decatur will bring us to Tujaque's Restaurant. In the 1870s and 1880s this was the famous Madame Begue's Restaurant, frequented by workers in the French Market and elite Creole families for Sunday brunch. In *Saratoga Trunk*, Clio Dulaine (Ingrid Berman) and Clint Maroon (Gary Cooper) dine here.

Diagonally across the street, we can enjoy café au lait and beignets at Café du Monde. Wendall Rohr (Dustin Hoffman) in *Runaway Jury* savored this New Orleans version of coffee and doughnuts. We then walk up the stairs to a riverfront park area where the views of the Mississippi River and Jackson Square are spectacular. From here, we can see some of the old wharves along the river like the ones used in *Panic in the Streets*.

Andrew Jackson

UPPER QUARTER

We now enter Jackson Square (1721) where the equestrian statue of General Andrew Jackson (1856) brings to mind the Battle of New Orleans depicted in *The Buccaneer*. This landscaped park is the heart of the French Quarter and is a favorite place of filmmakers. It was once a military parade ground during the French and Spanish colonial periods. We have a good view of the St. Louis Cathedral (1851), the Cabildo (1799) (townhall) to the left of the Cathedral, and the Presbytére (1789) (literally priests' house) to the right of the Cathedral. The Cabildo and Presbytére are now parts of the Louisiana State Museums System with exhibits on the city's history and culture.

On either side of the Square are the Pontalba Buildings (1849-1850). Micaela Almonester Pontalba financed and oversaw the work on these buildings. The Baroness Pontalba is a legendary figure in New Orleans history. In the ironwork on the second floor verandas, you can see the initials "AP" representing her maiden and married names. She was a wealthy native of New Orleans who was married in the Cathedral and sailed to France where she and her husband lived in a chateau during their stormy relationship. The 1850s House in the Pontalba building to the right displays living quarters in keeping with that period and offers walking tours in the morning and afternoon sponsored by the Friends of the Cabildo (a volunteer group supporting the Louisiana State Museums).

We proceed through the Square and upon exiting turn to the left of the Cathedral (the interior is duplicated in *Saratoga Trunk*) and we look at the Café Pontalba (on the ground floor of the upriver Pontalba). This is where the judge in *Runaway Jury* treats the jury members to lunch. Also, during the Tennessee Williams Festival in March each year, the "Stella" calling contest mimicking Stanley's (Marlon Brando) cry to his wife Stella (Kim Hunter) in *A Streetcar Named Desire* takes place below the veranda of the Pontalba Building.

Stroll through Pirates Alley between the Cabildo and the Cathedral. This narrow alley, according to local lore, was a place where pirates met with local citizens to make deals. Halfway down the alley we stop at the Faulkner House (624 Pirates Alley). Nobel Laureate, William Faulkner, wrote his first novel, *Soldiers' Pay*, while living here and was inspired by the Quarter's 1920s ambience early in his career. In the film *Walk on the Wild Side*, Dove (Laurence Harvey) rents a second floor apartment here for Hallie (Capucine) when he tries to rescue her from the Doll House. In *The Pelican Brief*, a funeral service for the Tulane law professor was filmed on the back steps of the Cathedral and in St. Anthony's Garden (the garden behind the Cathedral). According to the legend, duels in the city's early history took place in this garden.

14 We turn around toward the short alley leading to St. Peter Street (this is Cabildo Alley) and cross the street to 632 St. Peter where Tennessee Williams lived while writing the play which was made into the movie *A Streetcar Named Desire*. From his apartment window, he could hear the rumbling noise made by the Desire streetcar as it made its way through the French Quarter. Desire Street below the French Quarter is where the streetcar used to turn around. A Desire streetcar was on display at the back of the U.S. Mint on Esplanade Avenue for several years (See the sketch of the Desire streetcar).

15 We then proceed on Royal Street, and turn right, and walk to the intersection with Orleans Avenue. The Wyndam Bourbon Orleans Hotel on this street has a ballroom on the second floor where (according to local lore) Quadroon Balls like the one shown in *Feast of All Saints* were held. The staircase to the ballroom can be seen from the lobby of the hotel.

16 We turn back on Royal and walk upriver for two blocks to St. Louis Street. If we look to the right down St. Louis at the corner, we can see Antoine's Restaurant. This famous restaurant appears in *JFK, The Pelican Brief,* and *The Big Easy.* The main actors

8th District Police Station

in these movies dine at this restaurant.

17 Continuing past St. Louis on Royal, now we are in front of the Louisiana State Supreme Court Building. This Beaux Arts-style building (1910) was constructed on a square block where many historic structures once stood. The first two floors are covered with marble and the upper part with terra cotta designed to look like marble. The interior and exterior appear in *JFK* and *Runaway Jury*. The well-known Brennan's Restaurant is across the street.

18 Continue walking a half-block to the corner of Royal and Conti Streets. The Eighth District Police Station is where the detective Remy (Dennis Quaid) is stationed in *The Big Easy*. The police station was at one time the Bank of Louisiana (1826). This corner was once the banking center for the Creole population.

19 We turn left on Conti and left again on Chartres around the back of the Courthouse. We pass K-Paul's Louisiana Kitchen owned by the city's most celebrated Cajun chef, Paul Prudhomme. The original Maspero's Restaurant is on the corner of Chartres and St. Louis. On the wall, there is a tablet claiming that Andrew Jackson and Jean Lafitte (*The Buccaneer*) met here before the Battle of New Orleans. The historical fact is that Jackson and Lafitte did not meet here but could have met in several places in the Quarter. Tales like this one are part of New Orleans mythology, e.g. there is another plaque on the Old Absinthe House (240 Bourbon) telling about the two leaders having a rendezvous there.

🎥 **20** The Napoleon House across St. Louis Street is said to be where Napoleon would live if New Orleanians were successful in rescuing him from exile on St. Helena. The French Emperor was very popular among the local citizens of that time and some probably made a plan for his rescue which was never put into action. The bar is a favorite "watering hole" for writers, film stars, and other artists. Jim Garrison (Kevin Costner) in *JFK* watches the television coverage of the president's assassination here, and Rankin Fitch (Gene Hackman) in *Runaway Jury* drinks a cocktail at this bar. This is a good place to take a break.

🎥 **21** Directly across the street from the Napoleon House, we can see five arches which were part of the St. Louis Hotel (now part of the Royal Orleans Hotel). The St. Louis Hotel was duplicated on a Hollywood set for *Jezebel*. On that set, an elaborate bar with crystal chandeliers was constructed. This is where Preston (Henry Fonda) collapses as a victim of yellow fever. When the Royal Orleans Hotel (1960) was built, the preservation board, which oversees construction in the Quarter (the Vieux Carré Commission) convinced the contractors to put five arches from the St. Louis Hotel back where they once that this edifice was also known as the Exchange Hotel. A painting of the St. Louis Hotel by Boyd Cruise can be seen in the lobby of the Royal Orleans Hotel.

We turn left on St. Louis and proceed to Bourbon Street where we turn right and walk one block. Across Bourbon on the corner of Bourbon and Toulouse Streets is the Inn on Bourbon. It is on the site of the former French Opera House. In *Saratoga Trunk*, Clio (Ingrid Bergman) and Clint (Gary Cooper) go to the opera here. The indentation in the curb in front of the hotel was used as an off-the-street place for carriages that transported elegantly dressed women and men attending events at the Opera House. This grand building was the site of operas and Mardi Gras balls from 1859 until it burned to the ground in 1919. (See the sketch of the Opera House). We turn around and head back one block to St. Louis Street. If we look at the upper stories along Bourbon Street, we can imagine how this street was lined with fashionable townhouses and costume and set designers shops for the opera when the Opera House was in existence (1859-1919). Earl Long (Paul Newman) in *Blaze* meets Blaze Starr (Lolita Davidovitch) at a Bourbon Street nightclub. Blanche (Vivien Leigh) and Stella (Kim Hunter) go to Galatoire's Restaurant (209 Bourbon) for supper and then to a "show" (movie) in *A Streetcar Named Desire*.

When we reach St. Louis, we turn right and walk

Hermann-Grima House

A Streetcar Named Desire.

When we reach St. Louis, we turn right and walk to the Hermann-Grima House Museum (810 St. Louis). This 1831 house offers tours during which visitors see the living quarters, courtyard, kitchen, stable, and how rich families at that time lived. The Hermann-Grima House is used as a hotel in *Double Jeopardy*.

NEARBY THE FRENCH QUARTER

Fans of **Easy Rider** and counterculture history should take a tour of the St. Louis #1 Cemetery. It is recommended to take an organized tour with a group because caution should be observed when visiting this isolated and unguarded cemetery. "Save Our Cemeteries," listed in the telephone book, conducts tours on Sundays and other tour companies have tours during the week. Check with the receptionist at your hotel. The tours include stories about the Italian Benevolent Tomb where Captain America (Peter Fonda) in **Easy Rider** sits on the lap of a marble statue of a woman in one of the alcoves of the tomb (See the sketch of the tomb).

If we choose to take a cemetery tour, as we exit St. Louis #1, notice the brick wall. It is identical to the wall of St. Louis #2 cemetery which appears in the opening scene in **The Cincinnati Kid** when Eric (Steve McQueen) passes as a jazz funeral led by the Eureka Brass Band comes out of that cemetery. Also, there is an orange colored brick building on the corner of Basin and Bienville Streets one block away with a sign "Basin Street Super Market." This structure was part of Lula White's Annex, a brothel in notorious Storyville. **Pretty Baby** is set in "the District" as Storyville was also called. The new Basin Station next to St. Louis #1

Italian Benevolent Society Tomb

is a good place to take a break. It has water fountains and rest rooms.

The last numbered stop on the tour map is where the Louisville and Nashville Passenger Terminal once stood. This stop on Canal Street and the River is 18 blocks away. We may want to save it for another time. The Canal Street streetcar travels to the foot of the River. The first scene in *A Streetcar Named Desire* was shot at the train terminal. From there, we can also see Spanish Plaza at the foot of Canal Street. Parts of *The Pelican Brief* and *Runaway Jury* were filmed in that plaza. The paddle-wheeler, *The Creole Queen*, docks there and travels downriver to Chalmette Battlefield Park where we can picture the Battle of New Orleans as portrayed in *The Buccaneer*. The nearby Algiers Ferry is free for pedestrians and gives passengers a panoramic view of the Mississippi. In a scene in *The Cincinnati Kid*, Eric (Steve McQueen) and Shooter (Karl Malden) ride on a ferry on the river and look toward the city's skyline, now considerably modernized. While at Spanish Plaza, we can see the two bridges of the Crescent City Connection crossing the Mississippi. These bridges appear in *Runaway Jury* and in *Déjà Vu* (a movie featuring Denzel Washington).

Now that we have completed the French Quarter Tour, we have an appreciation for the compact size of the Quarter. The old Creole neighborhood is the oldest part of the city. It is on high ground created by the Mississippi River. The St. Charles Avenue streetcar tour travels through another strip of high ground in the American sector, also elevated by soil deposited by the River. Certainly, the city's founders knew what they were doing when settling along the high ground.

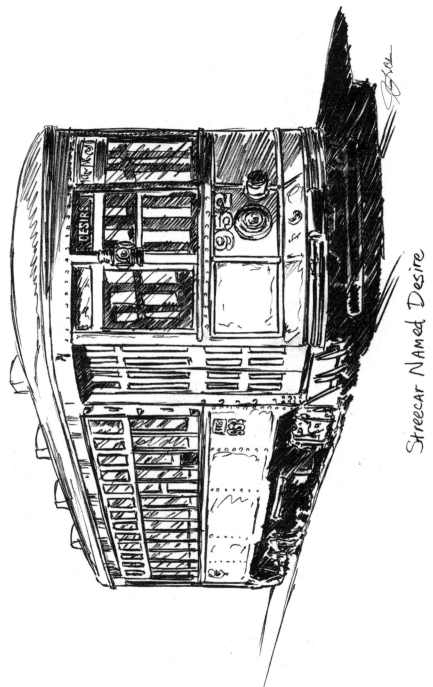

Streecar Named Desire

STREETCAR TOUR OF MOVIE SITES ON ST. CHARLES AVENUE

A VisiTour pass gives us an unlimited number of rides on all streetcar and bus lines for $5 a day or $12 for three days. These passes are available at VisiTour vendors. Ask the desk at the hotel about these passes. Fares for streetcars and buses are currently $1.25 in exact change. On the St. Charles streetcar, we have to pay $1.25 when we board the car and another $1.25 to return and if we stop somewhere along the line, we have to pay the fare again upon boarding. We catch the historic St. Charles streetcar at the corner of Canal and Carondelet Streets. It takes 90 minutes to ride from Canal Street to the end of the line at Carrollton and Claiborne Avenues.

The green metal streetcars with wooden seats, brass hardware, and open windows running on the St. Charles line are identical to the Desire streetcars made internationally famous in *A Streetcar Named Desire*. Passengers can get off at different stops by pulling the overhead cord before reaching a stop. The St. Charles tracks wind their way through the Central Business District and on to a grass-covered route under a canopy of live oak trees, past picturesque homes, churches, and schools. This streetcar line takes us back in time to when the wealthy American sector was experiencing a golden age. The line dates back to 1835 and used to take people from the edge of the French Quarter (a Creole neighborhood) to the Garden District and other parts of the premiere English-speaking neighborhood of the old city.

Once aboard the streetcar, we can see why the New Orleans streetcars are immortalized in films. How did Blanche Du Bois (Vivien Leigh) feel when she rode on the Desire line to Kowalski's apartment on Elysian Fields Avenue? Director Elia Kazan, as we saw earlier, brought Vivien Leigh to the city in late October to shoot the opening sequences in the film *A Streetcar Named Desire*. When the film crew was in place on Canal Street in front of the Louisville and Nashville train station (this station was at the foot of Canal Street near the river, see #25 on the French Quarter tour), city officials ran a Desire car past this location (the Desire line had been replaced by buses in 1948). The appearance of a Desire streetcar re-creates a magical moment in the movie's story and sets the tone for the rest of the picture (this could not be done on the Broadway stage).

In the cinema world, the streetcar is to New Orleans what the cable car is to San Francisco. In reality, streetcars in New Orleans are icons to its people. In the city's history, the population has displayed an indomitable spirit and joy of life (*joie de*

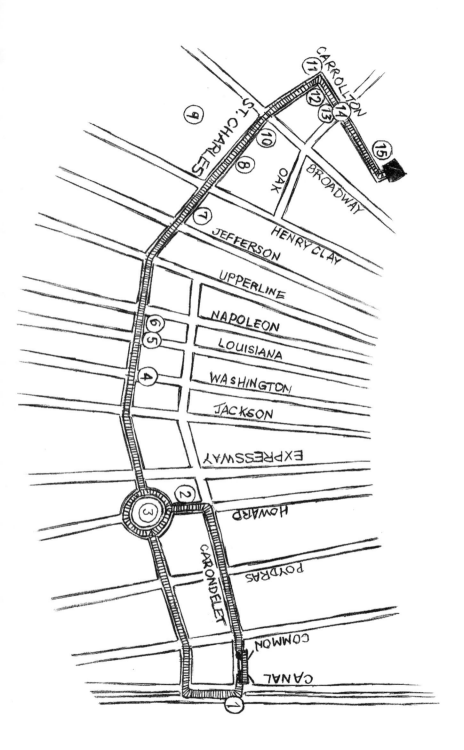

vivre) in the face of disasters. From the beginning in 1718, the city recovered from floods, hurricanes, fires, and epidemics. Most recently, the St. Charles streetcar line was restored after three years of work at a cost of $13 million following Hurricane Katrina.

A ride on this route allows us to experience the city's resilience. This line was used in **Runaway Jury** when Marlee (Rachel Weiz) tricks Rankin Fitch (Gene Hackman) into boarding a car on Canal Street as he exits the Palace Café Restaurant while pursuing her. Marlee knows that he cannot identify her when both of them are on a crowded streetcar. She tells him her demands for swaying the jury he is trying to control, and then jumps off the car after telling him that the next stop is the Audubon Zoo. The persons on the streetcar in the movie are commuters who ride to and from work. As shown in that film, on our ride we will see a similar group of commuters. The map marks film sites and other points of interest along the way. Enjoy the slow pace of the journey!

St. Charles is named for Carlos III who ruled Spain when Louisiana was a Spanish colony. When the streetcar enters the Central Business District, bear in mind that this was the first English-speaking section and Canal Street was the commons or "neutral ground" between the Americans and the French-speaking Creoles in the Vieux Carré. The shipping trade in New Orleans, especially when steamboats started to come to port, created a prosperous American merchant class. Many businesses and banks were opened here by this group. Homes, theaters, hotels, and bars were also built in this area. The rivalry between the two cultures manifested itself in the 1800s when the American sector established churches and a public square, which was ironically named for the Marquis de Lafayette, the French hero of the American Revolutionary War who visited the city in 1825. Thus, Lafayette Square became the heart of the American part of the city, while *Place d'Ames* in the French Quarter became Jackson Square to honor Andrew Jackson, the American hero of the Battle of New Orleans.

Two blocks past Poydras Street (the first wide cross street on the line), we can see Lafayette Square on the left and on the right, Gallier Hall (formerly the City Hall). Gallier Hall is one of the finest examples of Greek Revival architecture in the United States. Built in 1845, it symbolizes the ascendance of the Americans in New Orleans. The Mayor of the City still toasts Rex on Mardi Gras day from a stand in front of this hall.

Lafayette Square appears in *Panic in the Streets* and *JFK*. The actors in the leading roles in these two pictures, Richard Widmark and Kevin Costner, meet with other characters in this park. The Lafayette Hotel adjacent to the Square is where the high stakes poker game in the storyline of *The Cincinnati Kid* takes place.

Lee Circle. A statue of Robert E. Lee stands on top of a tall granite column here. New Orleans was captured in 1862 when a Union flotilla fought its way up the Mississippi River from the Gulf of Mexico. In the film, *Band of Angels* (1957) (not covered in the book), starring Clark Gable, Yvonne DeCarlo, and Sidney Poitier, the city's surrender and its occupation are depicted in a costume epic based on Robert Penn Warren's novel of the same name. Even though New Orleans fell in the first year of the Civil War, it remained loyal to the Confederacy, despite its long occupation (1862-1877) by federal troops. The Lee monument erected in 1884 is a testament to that loyalty.

The land past Lee Circle used to be part of several plantations. As we proceed on the streetcar, there are many mansions along the way that are reminiscent of plantation houses such as Julie's (Bette Davis') home, Halcyon, in *Jezebel*. The streetcar runs parallel to the Mississippi River until it reaches the Riverbend area where it turns off of St. Charles Avenue on to Carrollton Avenue.

One block away from Lee Circle, the large multi-colored brick building on the right is the Jerusalem Temple. It served as the headquarters of the Shriners, and is now a church. The first streets ahead are named for muses in Greek mythology, e.g. Clio, Melpomene, and Terpsichore. This section is known as the Lower Garden District.

Eleven blocks upriver from the Jerusalem Temple, on the right, is the Ponchartrain Hotel. It was a traditional uptown hotel and is now an apartment building. (Writers Tennessee Williams and Walker Percy lived here at different times.)

In the same block on the left on the corner of St. Charles and Josephine Street, we can see "a piece of Paris," i.e. a part of the Eiffel Tower. A catering business is housed in what was an upper-level restaurant in the Eiffel Tower in Paris. It was built in 1936 and later removed for structural reasons, stored in a warehouse, and moved and reassembled as a restaurant in New Orleans in 1986.

Washington Avenue. Six blocks after Jackson Avenue is Washington Avenue. This is a good place to take a break. After getting off the streetcar, we walk one block toward the river on Washington. The Rink on the corner of Prytania and Washington is a small shopping center housing several stores. A coffee shop here has refreshments and restrooms. A Garden District tour with an experienced guide is recommended. Such a tour can be booked in advance at hotels. These tours include stops at Anne Rice's former home and Lafayette Cemetery #1. Several Hollywood productions used the cemetery for a filming location. In **Double Jeopardy**, the main character Libby (Ashley Judd) is knocked unconscious and put into a tomb. The prop supervisors in the

Columns Hotel

picture built an above-ground tomb for this sequence in the movie. A Garden District tour usually takes about two hours.

If we chose to get off the streetcar at Washington Avenue, we pay the fare (presently $1.25 in exact change) or use a VisiTour pass.

Eight blocks from Washington Avenue on the left on the corner of Louisiana Avenue is the former House of Bultman Funeral Home. This is now a Borders Bookstore, but the façade to the original building has been preserved. The two-story solarium in the residence directly behind the bookstore on Louisiana Avenue was used as a model for the play and movie, **Suddenly, Last Summer** (1959) set in 1930s New Orleans. Tennessee Williams lived in this house for a month and may have been inspired to use this locale.

Five blocks upriver on the right is the Columns Hotel. A large part of **Pretty Baby** (1978) was filmed here. Almost all of the interior scenes were shot inside the hotel. The first floor of the hotel looks like a set for the movie.

Six blocks upriver on the street, we come to Napoleon Avenue (named for Emperor Napoleon). The most famous Mardi Gras parades begin at Napoleon and St. Charles Avenues. Leading to this intersection, we see beads in the wires and trees. These are some of

the throws from floats in the parades using this route. Also, we begin to see joggers on the "neutral ground" (median). This tells us that we are near the university area. After crossing Napoleon, on the right in the second block is the Academy of the Sacred Heart (a famous Catholic girl's school). Five blocks ahead on the right, we see the Orléans Club, a venerable women's club.

In the next block on the left, the Milton H. Latter Memorial Library was at one time a private residence. Marguerite Clark (1883-1940), a star on stage and in silent films (*Wildflower* and *Snow White*), lived here in the 1920s. The library on this full square belongs to the city, though its future as a library is uncertain.

In the fifth block, after the Latter Library on the right, on the corner of Arabella and St. Charles, is the Palmer House. This is the only real "Tara" in existence. The architects designed it to look like "Tara" on the set of *Gone With the Wind* (1939). "Tara" on the Hollywood backlot was torn down after the picture was completed.

Five blocks ahead on the right, are Loyola and Tulane Universities. Parts of *The Pelican Brief* (1993) were filmed at Tulane in the former Law School Building on Freret Street toward the back of the campus.

Audubon Park on the left is one of the city's two

largest parks. The zoo near the river in the park served as a location for **Cat People** (1982). This was before the zoo underwent extensive remodeling. Now it is one of the nation's best zoological parks.

On the right after passing Tulane, we see Audubon Place. Tom Cruise and his wife at that time, Nicole Kidman, rented a home on this private street during the making of **Interview With the Vampire** (1994).

Riverbend. As the streetcar turns on to Carrollton Avenue, there is a pleasant view of the levee on the river. This is a good place to take a break. There are several popular restaurants and cafés here. Camellia Grill is one. This building with large white pillars on the front has an Old South look.

In the second block on the right, the large Greek Revival structure was the Courthouse of Jefferson Parish before the turn of the twentieth century. The town of Carrollton and this vicinity was annexed by Orleans Parish. At present, the building is a public school.

In the fourth block after this building, on the right are two houses notable for their architectural aesthetics which could be used in films. One is a Gothic Revival house at 1015 Carrollton and the other is a Colonial Revival house at 1031 Carrollton. The next street crossing Carrollton is Oak Street.

14 When we look to the left on Oak, we get a glimpse of the shops on that street. These stores were used to represent the 1930s in the movie *All the King's Men* (the 2006 re-make of the 1949 classic film based on Robert Penn Warren's Pulitzer-winning novel of the same name). Willy Stark, the central character, is a fictionalized political leader modeled after Louisiana's Huey Long. Broderick Crawford and Sean Penn, respectively, play this role in the two films. Also, the former bank building with a large clock appears in the 2008 picture, *The Curious Case of Benjamin Butler*, starring Brad Pitt and Cate Blanchette. A scene in that film shows the streetcar passing Oak Street. The movie comes from a short story written by F. Scott Fitzgerald about a man who experiences reverse-aging.

15 On the left, in the third block after Oak, we are able to see the Willow Street Streetcar Barn. This is where the cars are repaired and housed. Again, the fabled Desire streetcar as portrayed in the play and movie comes to mind.

The St. Charles ride continues for ten blocks until it reaches the end of the tracks at Claiborne Avenue. On the left here is Palmer Park (a large neighborhood park). Passengers can ride back to Canal Street after paying another fare or using a VisiTour pass.

END NOTES

Chapter 1 – Why New Orleans has attracted films

"A courtesan, not old"; *William Faulkner, New Orleans Sketches,* edited by Carvel Collins (New York : Random House, 1958). 13.

Chapter 2 – The Colonial Period – 1718-1810

"it comes not only from reading of all the literature"; *Interview With the Vampire,* Anne Rice (New York : Random House, 1976). 148.

Chapter 3 – The Free People of Color – 1809-1850

"Yet in their shadowy world"; *The Feast of All Saints,* Anne Rice (New York : Simon & Schuster, 1979). 8.

Chapter 4 – The Americanization Era – 1803-1840

"By the Eternal"; *The Battle of New Orleans,* Robert V. Remini (New York : Viking Pres, 1999). 70. Chapter 5 – Jezebel in the French Quarter – 1840-1877.

"Of course we were greatly"; *The Tumultuous Life* and *Times of the Omni Royal Orleans Hotel*, John DeMers (New Orleans : Omni Royal Orleans Hotel, 1993). 56.

Chapter 6 – Clio Dulaine in Posbellum New Orleans – 1865-1877

"You are – very beautiful"; *Saratoga Trunk*, Edna Ferber (Garden City, NY : Doubleday, 1941). 136.

"A New Orleans bitch";

Ingrid Bergman, My Story, Ingrid Bergman and Alan Burgess (New York : Delacote Press, 1980) 132.

"Oh, it's delicious"; *Saratoga Trunk*, 54-55.

"Yes, isn't it lucky?"; Ibid. 136.

"Take shame on yourself"; Ibid, 44.

"Mah mule is white"; Ibid, 39.

Chapter 7 – The Legacy of Storyville – 1898-1917

"The District"; *Storyville, New Orleans : Being an Authentic, Illustrated Account of the Notorious Red-Light District*, Al Rose (Tuscaloosa, AL : The University of Alabama

Press, 1974) ix.

Chapter 8 – Film in the Great Depression Era – 1918-1940s

"Negroes in purple"; *The WPA Guide to New Orleans* (New Orleans : Pantheon Books, 1983) xxxv.

Chapter 10 – A Streetcar Named Desire – The 1950s

"Whoever you are"; *A Streetcar Named Desire,* Tennessee Williams (New York : New Directions Book, 1947) 170.

"We used the city's people"; *Elia Kazan, A Life.* Elia Kazan (New York : Knopf, 1988) 379.

"I learned for instance"; Ibid, 380-381.

"I'd get out of that"; Ibid. 384.

"Kazan Street"; see *When Blanche Met Brando,* Sam Staggs (New York ; St. Martin's Press. 2005) 155.

"I would shoot Blanche's arrival"; *Elia Kazan, A Life,* Ibid, 384.

"They told me to take a streetcar": *A Streetcar Named Desire,* Ibid,
"I'd make the old city's presence": *Elia Kazan, A Life,* Ibid, 384.

"I particularly remember"; Ibid, 385.

Chapter 11 – Hollywood is Transformed – 1969-1970s

"We did it man": transcribed from the video recording *Easy Rider*, for an account of what happened when the film was being made see *Easy Riders, Raging Bulls : How the Sex-Drugs and Rock N' Roll Generation Saved Hollywood,* Peter Biskin (New York : Simon & Schuster, 1998).

Chapter 12 – A City of Music – A Timeless Tradition

"Just relax, darling"; transcribed from the video recording *The Big Easy*.

Chapter 13 – Conspiracy Movies in New Orleans

"The ghost of John F. Kennedy"; *JFK, The Book of the Film,* Oliver Stone and Zachary Sklar (New York : Applause Books, 1992) 176-177.

BIBLIOGRAPHY

Anderson, Sherwood, *Memoirs, A Critical Edition*. Newly edited from the original manuscripts by Ray Lewis White, Chapel Hill, NC : University of North Carolina Press, 1967.

Algren, Nelson, *A Walk on the Wild Side*, New York : Farrar, Strass and Cudahy, 1956.

Biskind, Peter, *Easy Riders, Raging Bulls : How the Sex-Drugs and Rock N' Roll Generation Saved Hollywood,* New York : Simon & Schuster, 1998.

Cahir, Linda Costanza, *Literature into Film : Theory and Practical Approaches,* Jefferson, NC : McFarland & Company Inc. Publishers, 2006.

Corrigan, Timothy J., *A Short Guide to Writing About Film,* New York : Pearson-Longman, Sixth Edition, 2007.

DeMers, John, *French Quarterly Royalty : The Tumultuous Life and Times of the Omni Royal Orleans Hotel,* New Orleans, LA : Omni Royal Orleans Hotel, 1993.

Ferber, Edna, *Saratoga Trunk,* Garden City, NY : Doubleday, 1941.

Galsworthy, John, *The Inn of Tranquility : Studies and Essays,* New York : Schribner, 1912.

Gehman, Mary, *The Free People of Color : An Introduction,* New Orleans, LA : Margaret Media, Inc., 1994

Grisham, John, *The Pelican Brief,* New York : Island Books, 1993.

_____, *The Runaway Jury,* New York : Doubleday, 1996

Heard, Malcolm, *French Quarter Manual : An Architectural Guide to New Orleans' Vieux Carré,* Jackson, MS : University Press of Mississippi, 1997.

Reeves, Tony, *The Worldwide Guide to Movie Locations,* Chicago, IL : A Capella Books, 2001.

Rice, Anne, *The Feast of All Saints,* New York: Simon & Schuster, 1979.

_____, *Interview With the Vampire,* New York : Random House, 1976.

Staggs, Sam, *When Blanche Met Brando, The Scandalous Story of A Streetcar Named Desire,* New York : St. Martin's Press, 2005.

Stone, Oliver and Zachary Sklar, *JFK: The Book of the Film,* New York: Applause Books, 1992.

The W.P.A. Guide to New Orleans, New Orleans, LA : The Historic New Orleans Collection, 1983 (Reprint of the 1938 WPA Guide with a new introduction).

Williams, Tennessee, *Vieux Carré,* New York : New Directions Publications, 1979.

Wilson, Samuel, Jr., "The Vieux Carré of New Orleans: Its Plan, Its Growth, Its Architecture" in *Plan and Program for the Preservation of the Vieux Carré,* 9-37, New Orleans, LA : Bureau of Governmental Research, 1968.

1018 Royal St.

LIST OF ALL MOVIES SET IN NEW ORLEANS

SOME FILMED IN THE CITY, SOME FILMED IN STUDIOS, SOME FILMED IN BOTH

TV-Made for TV, V- Made as a Video

Above & Beyond (2001)

Adventures of Captain Fabian (1951)

After Katrina : Rebuilding St. Bernard Parish (2006)

After the Storm (2008)

Albino Alligator (1996)

All Dogs Go to Heaven (1989)

All on a Mardi Gras Day (2003)

All the King's Men (2006)

Always for Pleasure (1978)

American Beer (2004)

American Can, The (2008)

American Creole Reunion (2006) TV

American Heritage of Hospitality (1949)

American Mormon (2005) V

American Standards, The (2007)

American Summer (2008)

American Violet (2008)

American Opera, An (2007)

American Widow (2008)

Angel Heart (1987)

Angels Die Slowly (2008)

Animal Rescue Katrina (2006)V

Another Lost Angel (2008)

Arrival of Rex (1902)

At Last (2005)

Autopsy (2008)

Bad City Blues (1999)

Bad Lieutenant : Port of Call New Orleans (2009)

Badge, The (2002)

Baller Blockin' (2000)

Baltimore Bullet, The (1980)

Band of Angels (1957)

Banjo on My Knee (1936)

Bank + Shot (2007)

Baptized at Katrina :A Refuge of Last Resort (2006)

Bed of Roses (1933)

Been Down That Muddy Road : The Legend of Joe Barry (2007)

Before the Music Dies (2006)

Belle of New Orleans, The (1912)

Belle of the Nineties (1934)

Bi the Way (2008) [sic}

Birth of the Blues (1941)

Big Easy, The (1987)

Big Momma's House 2 (2006)

Black Saturday (2005) V

Black Soldier Blues (2006) TV

Black Water Transit (2008)

Blaze (1989)

Blue Chips (1994)

Bolden! (2008)

Bond 1973 : The Lost Documentary (1973)

Box Elder (2008)

Brad Paisley's Muddi Gras (2005) TV

Broken Promise (2006)

Brook Ellison Story, The (2004) TV

Buccaneer, The (1938)

Buccaneer, The (1958)

Buccaneer's Girl (1950)

Bucktown Romance, A (1912)

Bug (2006)

Bury the Hatchet (2008)

Butterfly, Butterfly (2009)

Call, The (2007)

Calling, The (2008)

Camino, El (2008)

Campus Capers (1942)

Candyman : Farewell to Flesh (1995)

Cat People (1982)

Chamber, The (1996)

Change (2002)

Chasing the Dream (2008)

Cheese (2009)

Chess (2009)

Child of Glass (1978) TV

Christmas Holiday (1944)

Cincinnati Kid, The (1965)

Cinerama Holiday (1955)

Circe the Enchantress (1924)

Client, The (1994)

Climbing Out (2002)

Code Name Silencer (1995)

College (2008)

Columbia Musical Travelark : Wonders of New Orleans (1957)

Continental Guards, The (1902)

Crazy in Alabama (1999)

Crossroads (2002)

Cry of the Werewolf (1944)

Crypt of Dark Secrets (1976)

Curious Case of Benjamin Button, The (2008)

Cut Up (1994)

Cypress Edge (1999)

D-Day the Ultimate Conflict (2004) TV

Damn show!, The (2005)

Damn Citizen (1958)

Dangerous, The (1994)

Dark Angel (1996) TV

Dark Waters (1944)

Dark Water Rising : Survival Stories of Hurricane Katrina Animal Rescues (2006)

DC Talk : Free at Last (2002) TV

Dead Dog (2000)

Dead Man on the Run (1975) TV

Dead Man Walking (1995)

Dead One, The (1961)

Dead Will Tell, The (2004) TV

Deadline (2009)

Deal (2008)

Dear Mr. President (2006)

Death Toll (2008)

Déjà Vu (2006)

Delta Heat (1992)

Desert Bayou (2007)

Desire and Hell at Sunset Motel (1992)

Difficult Death (2008)

Dixie (1943)

Dixiana (1930)

Docks of New Orleans, The (1948)

Don't Eat the Baby : Adventures of Post-

Katrina Mardi Gras (2007)

Double Jeopardy (1999)

Doublecrossed (1991) TV

Down by the Law (1986)

Dracula 2000 (2000)

Drowning Pool, The (1975)

Down in Dixie (2006)

Duel on the Mississippi (1955)

Dukes of Hazzard, The (2005)

Dummy, The (1995)

Easy Rider (1969)

Elvis (2005) TV

Employee Dang (2003)

Evil in the Bayou (2003) V

Exit to Eden (1994)

Factory Girl (2006)

Failure to Launch (2006)

Fait Accompli (1998)

Faith of My Fathers (2005) TV

False Witness (1989) TV

Faubourg Treme : The Untold Story of Black New Orleans (2008)

Fantastic Four (2005)

Father Hood (1993)

Father of Lies (2007)

Faustbook (2006) V

Fay Wray : A Life (2008)

Feast of All Saints, The (2004)

Felony (1996)

Feral (2006)

Fields of Fuel (2008)

Fighting Kentuckian, The (1949)

Final Cut (1993)

Final Destination 4 (2009)

Fire Next Time, The
(1993) TV

First 9 ½ Weeks, The
(1998)

Five Fingers (2006)

Fix, The (2006)

Flakes (2007)

Flame of New Orleans
(1941)

Flat Daddy (2007)

Flesh and Fantasy (1943)

For One Night (2006) TV

Four for the Morgue
(1963)

Foxes of Harrow (1947)

Frankenstein (2004) TV

French Quarter (1977)

French Quarter
Undercover (1986)

French Silk (1994) TV

Friends of the Family II
(1996)

From the Mouthpiece
Back (2008)

Gabriel Knight : Sins of
the Fathers (1993)

Gambler from Natchez
(1954)

Getting It Together : the
Willie Metcalf Story
(1999)

Ghost Trip (2001)

Ghost Writers (2000)

Ginny Owens : Live in
New Orleans (2005) V

Girl in Trouble (1963)

Give the Anarchist a
Cigarette (2005)

Glass Cage, The (1996)

Glass Houses (2008)

Glory Alley (1952)

Glory at Sea (2008)

Glory Road (2006)

Going Overboard (1989)

Grand Isle (1991)

Great Observer, The (2008)

Greetings from Out Here (1993)

Ground Truth : After the Killing Ends, The (2006)

Growing Pains : Return of the Seavers (2004) TV

Guardian, The (2006)

Gun in Betty Lou's Handbag, The (1992)

Gus and Rose : Reflections of Hurricane Katrina (2007) V

Hail Columbia (1935)

Hall of Mirrors (2001)

Halloween Havoc (1993) V

Handy Andy (1934)

Hard N' Heavy Volume II (1990) V

Hard Target (1993)

Hard Times (1975)

Hatchet (2006)

Haunted Mansion, The (2003)

Heartless II (2005/1) TV

Heaven's Prisoners (1996)

Hello Sister, Goodbye Life (2006) TV

Hellp (2006) [sic]

Her Sister's Secret (1946)

Highway 61 (1991)

His Turning Point (1915)

Hitman :Blood Money (2006)

Hobson's Choice (1983) TV

Holdout (2006)

Holiday for Sinners (1952)

Home of Phobia (2004)

Hotel (1967)

House of Secrets (1993) TV

Hurricane Party (2008)

Hurricane Season (2008)

Hurricanes: On the Brink (2006)

I Love You Phillip Morris (2009)

In the Electric Mist (2008)

In the Wake (2007)

Infidelity (2004) TV

Interview With the Vampire : The Vampire Chronicles (1994)

Invisible Avenger, The (1958)

Iron Mistress (1952)

Jackass Number Two (2006)

Jake Lassiter : Justice on the Bayou (1995) TV

Jezebel (1938)

Jimmy Carter : Man from Plains (2007)

Jitterbugs (1943)

JKF (1991)

JFK Assassination : The Jim Garrison Tapes (1992)

J.D's Revenge (1976)

John Petticoats (1919)

Johnny Angel (1945)

Johnny Handsome (1989)

Josette (1938)

Judas Kiss (1998)

Judges : Devil's Bayou (2010)

Jugular Wine : A Vampire Odyssey (1994)

Just My Luck (2006)

Katrina's Children (2008)

Katrina's Wake (2006)

Keep Off My Grass (1975)

Kill Theory (2008)

King Creole (1958)

Labou (2006)

Lady From Louisiana (1941)

Land of Opportunity : The Mardi Gras (1950)

Last of the Buccaneers (1950)

Larry Keel : Beautiful Thing (2004) V

Last Holiday (2006)

Last Night of the Mardi Gras (2003)

Last of the Mobile Hot Shots (1970)

Last Time (2006)

Leestemaker : Portrait of an Artist (2003)

Leningrad Cowboys Go America (1989)

Let the Good Times Roll Again (2007) TV

Let's Do It Again (1975)

Let's Eat Lolly (2009)

Letters from a Killer (1998)

Librarian : The Curse of Judas Chalice, The (2008) TV

Life Is Not a Fairytale : The Fantasia Barrino Story (2006) TV

Lifestyle, The (1999)

Little Chevalier, The (2008)

Little Chenier (2008)

Live and Let Die (1973)

Living Proof (2008) TV

Loading a Mississippi Steamboat (1898)

Local Color (2006)

Locusts (2005) TV

Lolita (1997)

Loud Color, A (2006)

Louisiana (1984) TV

Louisiana Blues (1993)

Louisiana Hussy (1959)

Louisiana Purchase

(1941)

Louisiana Territory
  (1953)

Love & Suicide (2006) V

Love Liza (2002)

Love Song for Bobby Long,
  A (2004)

Low and Behold (2007)

Macabro (1980)

Mad Money (2008)

Madame's Family : The
  Truth About the Canal
  Street Brothel, The
  (2004) TV

Make It Funky! (2005)

Make It Happen (2008)

Malchance (2004)

Malpractice (2001)

Marching with the Saints
  (2006)

Mardi Gras (1958)

Mardi Gras (2009)

Mardi Gras Carnival
  (1898/I)

Mardi Gras Carnival
  (1898/II)

Mardi Gras Massacre
  (1978)

Mardi Gras Parade
  (1902)

Mardi Gras : Made in
  China (2005)

Margarita Bowl (1997)
  TV

Mary (2007)

Masking, The (2008)

Maxed Out : Hard Times,
  Easy Credit and the
  Era of Predatory
  Lenders (2006)

Memoirs from the City
  Care Forgot (2008)

Method (2004)

Miller's Crossing (1990)

Miracle Run (2004) TV

Mirrors (1978)

Mississippi Gambler, The (1953)

Modern New Orleans (1940)

Monster and the Stripper, The (1968)

Mr. 3000 (2004)

MTV Mardi Gras 2002 (2002) TV

MTV Mardi Gras 2003 (2003) TV

Murder at the Mardi Gras (1978) TV

Murder of Crows, A (1999) V

Music Rising (2006) TV

Mutiny (1998)

Mystery of the Riverboat, The (1944)

Napoleonic (2008) TV

National Vampire (2006)

Naughty Marietta (1935)

Naughty New Orleans

(1954)

Netherworld (1992)

Nevada Smith (1966)

New Moon (1940)

New Orleans (1947)

New Orleans After Dark (1958)

New Orleans Music in Exile (2006)

New Orleans Story (2008)

New Orleans Uncensored (1955)

New Orleans, Mon Amour (2008)

Next Exit, Main Street (2008)

Night in New Orleans (1942)

Night of Bloody Horror (1969)

Night of the Strangler (1972)

Night Trap (1993)

Nightmare (1956)

Nightmare Honeymoon (1973)

No Cross, No Crown (2008)

No Exit (2008)

No Mercy (1986)

No More Joy : The Rise and Fall of New Orleans Movie Theatres (2005) V

No Place Like Home (2006/II)

NOPD After Katrina (2005) TV

Nora Jones Lives in New Orleans (2003) V

Not Broken (2007)

Now You See It... (2005) TV

Number One (1969)

Nutria (2003)

Obsession (1976)

Odd Girl Out (2005) TV

Oil Storm (2005) TV

Old Louisiana (1937)

Old New Orleans (1940)

On Hostile Ground (2000) TV

Once Was Lost (2008)

One World (2001)

One : Chabad's Rescue and Relief Efforts in the Wake of Several Natural Disasters (2005) V

Operation Home Delivery (2006) TV

Order of the Garter, The (1999)

Panic in the Streets (1950)

Panoramic View of the French Market (1902)

Paper Roses (1997)

Paranoia (2008)

Party Police : Mardi Gras

(2007) TV

Payoff, The (1935)

Pelican Brief, The (1993)

Perennial Favorites (1998) V

Perfect Day, A (2006) TV

Peter Jennings Reporting : The Kennedy Assassination- Beyond Conspiracy (2003) TV

Piano Players Rarely Even Play Together (1982)

Pizza My Heart (2005) TV

Place to Dance, A (2005)

Playing for Change (2003)

Point of No Return (1993)

Poncho Sanchez : Keeper of the Flame (2007)

Pop Rocks (2004) TV

Popular Science (1943/I)

Premonition (2007/I)

Preparing for Thrusting (2008) V

Pretty Baby (1978)

Pride (2007)

Primary Colors (1998)

Prison Ball (2004)

Prom, The (2009)

Putting the River in Reverse (2006)

Quadroon (1972)

Queen of Apollo (1970)

Quincy & Althea (2007)

Racing for Time (2008) TV

Raw (2002)

Raw Justice (1994)

Ray (2004)

Reaping, The (2007)

Red Kimona, The (1925)

Refuge of Last Resort (2006) V

Resurrection (1999)

Revolution Green (2007)

Rhythm 'n' Bayous : A
   Road Map to Louisiana
   Music (2000)

Riders (2001)

Rise of the Undead (2005)
   V

Road, The (2008)

Robosapien Rebooted
   (2009)

Royal Rumble (2001)

Runaway Jury (2003)

Saratoga Trunk (1945)

Satchmo the Great (1957)

Savage Bees, The (1976)
   TV

Say Yes Quickly (2004)

Scarlet Saint (1925)

Scenic Highway (2006)

Season Before Spring
   (2008)

Second Line, The (2007)

Second Sight (2008)

Secret Kingdom, The
   (1998)

Shame on You (2010)

Shed (2005)

Sherlock Holmes : The
   Awakened (2007)

Shooting Gallery (2005) V

Sinners & Saints (2008)

Skeleton Key, The (2005)

Snatched (2010)

Snow Wonder (2005) TV

Solstice (2008) V

Song of the Vampire
   (2001) V

Sonny (2002)

Sonny Boy (2004)

Southern Fried Bigfoot
   (2007)

Spirit (2001) TV

Sporting Duchess, The (1920)

Spring Break '83 (2008)

Spring in New Orleans (1976) TV

Springtime (1914)

St. Francisville Experiment, The (2001)

Staircase Murders, The (2000) TV

Stay Alive (2006)

Stitches (2008)

Storm Stories : A Hurricane Katrina Anniversary Special (2006) TV

Storyville (1992)

Streetcar Named Desire, A (1951)

Stuck in the Suburbs (2004) TV

Suddenly, Last Summer (1959)

Summer Light (2002)

Sunny (1941)

Superdome (1978) TV

Supertanker (1980)

Surface Calm (2001)

Swamp Woman (1941)

Swamp Women (1955)

Tarnished Angels, The (1958)

Tennessee Williams' South (1973) TV

Thieves (2008)

This Gun for Hire (1991) TV

Three Days to Vegas (2007)

Tightrope (1984)

Tim's Island (2006)

Toast of New Orleans, The (1950)

Torn Apart (2004)

Torpedo Boat 'Dupont' (1898)

Tour the Set with Ike Barinholtz (2008) V

Toys in the Attic (1963)

Traveling Man (1989) TV

Trespassing (2004)

Tribe TV (1997) TV

Trouble the Water (2008)

Truth in Terms of Beauty (2007)

Tulia (2008)

Tune in Tomorrow (1990)

Turning Keys Over to Rex (1902)

Tuscaloosa (2008)

Two Smart People (1946)

Tyranny (2008)

Undercover Blues (1993)

Underground 2 (2004)

Unholy, The (1988)

Unnatural Disaster (2006)

Until Death (2007)

Unwilling Hero, An (1921)

Upperhand Cons (2009)

Vampire Bats (2005) TV

Vampyres (2007)

Vendetta (1999)

Venom (2005)

Voodoo Moon (2005) TV

Voodoo Music Experience 2003 (2003) TV

Voodoo Tailz (2002) TV

Wacky World of Dr. Morgus, The (1962)

Wade in the Water (2008)

Waiting (2008)

Wake, The (2007)

Walking Madison (2008)

Walk on the Wild Side (1962)

War Zone (1998)

Way Down South (1939)

Waters, The (2009)

Weather Paparazzi (2006) TV

Weeding by Example (2007)

Welcome Home Roscoe Jenkins (2008)

Welcome to Academia (2008)

Welcome to New Orleans (2006) TV

When I Was a Boy (1993)

When the Levees Broke: A Requiem in Four Acts (2006) TV

White Youth (1920)

Wild at Heart (1990)

Windjammer (1958)

Without Fear (2008)

Wormwood (1915)

WUSA (1970)

Zandelee (1991)

Zero Tolerance (1993)

INDEX

BIOGRAPHIES

Alan T. Leonhard is a native of New Orleans. He holds a B.A. and M.A. from Tulane University and a Ph.D. from Duke University in political science. While teaching at the university level for over thirty years, he received several grants for research and advanced studies including one from the National Endowment for the Humanities. He is also the author of many academic publications.

After retiring from the faculty of the University of New Orleans, he pursued a second profession as a tour guide and lecturer on the history of New Orleans. Upon completion of his initial training with the Friends of the Cabildo, a nationally recognized volunteer association supporting the Louisiana State Museum System, he started to conduct walking tours in the French Quarter. Over the years he has met many visitors who have formed stereotyped images of the city from motion pictures. These experiences led him to write *New Orleans Goes to the Movies.*

Jason Charles LeBlanc is also a native of New Orleans and currently resides there with his wife Aynsley and their two cats. Growing up an avid reader of graphic novels in addition to a predisposition to drawing, both sealed his "graphic" fate. A recipient of various artistic awards over his 14 year career, he has recently started his own business in graphic and fine art.